"Experience is th

Julius Caesar

GW00392300

The B2B Leaders Guidebook

Powerful tips, techniques and tools – all based on experience - to help you succeed in running a small B2B business, a start-up or a sales team in any size of business – all based on over 40 years of real-world business experience, including over 20 years in complex leadership roles.

Jim Irving

"I wear a suit of armour, made of my mistakes..."

Old French Proverb

The B2B Leaders Guidebook
First edition - 2020 by Jim Irving, distributed
in partnership with ebookpartnership.com
Copyright © Jim Irving 2020.

ISBN

This book is available in e-book, paperback
and audiobook formats.

Design by weareseventhree.com

Compendium

noun */kəmˊpen.di.əm/*

A detailed collection of information on a particular subject, especially in a short book...

Source: MacMillan Dictionary

About the Author

Jim was born in Edinburgh, Scotland and now lives in rural Northern Ireland with his wife, Yvonne. He has spent over 30 years in Business to Business (B2B) selling and business leadership in a number of tier one technology organisations including Amdahl, Sequent, Silicon Graphics (SGI) and Information Builders (www.ibi.com).

Over the last 14 years, since leaving the corporate world and starting his own consultancy, he has improved the sales processes and results and also mentored the business leaders in a large number of early stage and SME (Small to Medium Enterprise) organisations.

His career started with the hardest possible assignment – selling office equipment door to door in Scotland, in the depths of winter! His career rapidly developed into senior selling and sales leadership roles then ultimately to senior executive positions at major multinationals – including becoming the UK MD of Information Builders – a leading US based enterprise software company. At Silicon Graphics he was awarded the Corporation's 'Exemplary Leader' award. Jim has also held several executive marketing leadership posts. In recent years Jim has been both the Managing Director of an SME tech company and VP of sales and marketing for another. Of his 43 years' total business experience, he has spent over 20 years in direct management and leadership roles.

Jim has travelled extensively and worked in over 25 countries worldwide. He gained an MBA from Edinburgh Napier University in 1988. He is a Fellow of both the Chartered Institute of Marketing and The Institute,of Sales Management. He has spoken at a number of seminars and conferences and has in the past been an occasional visiting lecturer to both the Postgraduate Business school at Edinburgh Napier University and also to the Postgraduate Business School at Queens University, Belfast.

His first book, The B2B Selling Guidebook, has been highly successful. Positive comments from leading sales authors, positive reviews from The Institute of Sales Management and The Chartered Institute of Marketing, plus the specialist book reviews site 'Discovery' and consistent 5* Amazon reviews have quickly cemented his reputation as a writer.

When not working, Jim enjoys dining out, family time, running, travel, reading fiction and following current affairs.

Some Comments on Jim Irving as a Leader and Manager
(A fuller list is found in appendix 3)

"I worked with Jim whilst heading up pre-sales in a regional branch of a major US multinational. The branch had underperformed for several years and Jim was promoted to lead it. The change in style that Jim brought was questioned by some to start but over 2 years the region went from bottom in the UK to top and #2 in Europe. Jim's 'serving to lead' approach turned a group of individuals into a high performing team. It was incredibly effective."

Mike Robb, founder of independent IT consultancy, Avendris

"His no-frills, straightforward and ethical approach to building a world-class sales organization is something to this day that I not only admire, but also strive to emulate."

David Rode, Former Senior Vice President, International Operations, Information Builders Inc. (IBI)

"I first met Jim when I asked him to be the MD of a technology company I chaired. He brought clarity and strong execution to the business and massively increased market visibility while improving business results and motivating staff. He delivers very strong sales and communication skills to every endeavour."

Michael Black MBE, Successful technology entrepreneur. Non-Executive Director at Danske Bank, Non-Executive Director at Titan IC Systems and Chairman – Displaynote Technologies

"Jim is a natural sales leader, able to instantly command attention and respect from both his sales team and prospective clients. He has a relaxed and friendly approach which puts customers at ease and gains their trust. This, coupled with a keen commercial drive, enables him to identify opportunity, develop winning sales arguments and effectively manage the sales process to ensure his team make their numbers."

Ian Baxter, Former Vice President - NetDimensions

"Jim is a seasoned sales leader with a proven track record of success in multiple channels and business models. His leadership and motivation skills elevate the productivity of his teams resulting in consistently exceeded goals. He is respected by his customers, team, peers, and senior management."

Greg Goelz, President & CEO, Smart Locus Inc, California

A Sample of Feedback on The B2B Selling Guidebook
(A fuller list in appendix 2)

"Pick up a copy of this amazing enterprise selling book and break out the highlighters!!" I have just finished reading 'The B2B Selling Guidebook' by author Jim Irving. It is clear Jim is a big-time money-ball seller. His enterprise selling stories and business cases are moving and motivating. It is clear author Irving wants to leave something personal for the business community. His ideas are crystal clear and worth repeating. Pick up a copy and break out the highlighters!"

Patrick Tinney, world famous author of 'Perpetual Hunger' and other sales classics

"Jim Irving beats me. His 40+ years vs my 34 in B2B sales... Read it... regardless of your time served you will learn and you will be challenged... The B2B Selling Guide Book is so well thought through as Jim provides you with one insight and example after another. I really enjoyed the quotes, the lessons and the notes pages that turn this into a workbook to take around with you... This book takes its place in the PLAN. GROW. DO. Ltd recommendations that support our sales training."

Steve Knapp, The Sales Mindset Coach, author of "Funnel Vision

"Complete with an exclamation mark, 'keep learning' are the final two words of this excellent book by Jim Irving. Like a stick of Margate or Blackpool rock, those two words are weaved through all twenty-one chapters. Aimed at seasoned salespeople as well as novices, this little black book is a cornucopia of sales content and personal anecdotes from Jim's forty plus years in sales. The entire book is written in Plain English (a pleasant change) and there are some excellent appendices at the back. I'm reading this book again I liked it so much."

Jeremy Jacobs, The Sales Rainmaker

INSTITUTE OF SALES MANAGEMENT
"Irving writes in a clear, down to earth style. He is not so much teaching you but sharing ideas in the same way a sales manager might mentor a salesperson. Overall, it's a good read for any salesperson. Entrepreneurs looking to increase their sales will also find the book of value. The book is recommended for anyone looking for ideas on how to increase their knowledge about sales practice without a substantial time commitment."

ISM Winning Edge Magazine, July 2020. Reviewer – Roger Bradburn, COO and Director

CHARTERED INSTITUTE OF MARKETING

"In 'The B2B Selling Guidebook', Jim Irving sets out many of the fundamentals of professional and ethical selling. Jim is a CIM Fellow and a Fellow of the Institute of Sales Management. His 43-year career encompasses leadership roles in both disciplines. The book covers the most important sales lessons of his career. Each short, enjoyable chapter takes a sales attribute or discipline, explains it through real-life stories and then delivers insight to the reader." ... *with powerful lessons for all." www.cim.co.uk*

CIM Catalyst Magazine, July 2020 edition. Reviewer – John Knapton.

DISCOVERY BOOKS WEBSITE

"I found the format of this book unique and interesting... The author writes in simple language that makes it easy for people with no experience in sales to understand the subject. I think this makes the book a well-rounded work for anyone who wants to learn about B2B selling. I found this book informative, interesting and easy to understand."

Discovery Books, (see www.reedsy.com/discovery). Professional Reviewer – Satabdi Mukherjee

A Couple of the Many 5* Amazon Reviews

"Absolutely the most practical and useful book ever written on B2B selling. From beginning to end, Jim Irving's masterpiece is simplistically instructive but also captivating. This book is powered by Jim's 40+ years of selling experience. It's a shortcut through the hard knocks route of mastering the crazy nuances of the B2B selling profession. Highly recommend this book and this author."

Tkadams30 (USA)

"Regardless of your experience, you need this book. As a seasoned, long in the tooth sales professional and sales trainer, I have read a lot of stuff, mostly rubbish and one or two real gems. This book is in the latter category. Experienced sales professionals look to learn from other seasoned professionals for our development. We don't want theory; we want relatable experience that can be applied first hand. That's what you get in this book. In 2020 B2B sales needs to be effective, especially with Covid-19. This book felt like a safe pair of hands and I truly recommend you read it."

Simon Hares, SerialTrainer7 Ltd

**For Logan and DeeDee,
my beautiful Granddaughters**

Preface

"It takes a wise man to learn from his mistakes, but an even wiser man to learn from others."

Zen Proverb

This book is about the real world of leadership. It is based on my 43+ years career in business. I have seen the worst of managers; I have seen the best of leaders – and everything in between. My career took me to many countries and involved working alongside incredibly varied organisations and for small, medium and large employers. The latter part of my working life has seen me focus on helping start-ups, mostly those with a technology focus.

I have taken all of that experience and distilled it into this book. This is the second in my 'B2B' series. The first, 'The B2B Selling Guidebook' was very successful and opened many new and interesting doors for me. It also led to new friendships too. But it focussed on the individual salesperson, not the sales or business leader.

As I set out to write this book, I realised that I had gained very substantial experience in running (and in some cases, turning around) a broad mix of sales teams and then companies – some small, some very large. It is the accumulated 'team leading' experience and knowledge aspect that this book covers in detail. I have made many mistakes and I don't want you to drive into the same ditches that I did.

Who is this book for? Anyone who finds themselves managing and leading for the first time, particularly in small businesses, start-ups and in sales. It's equally relevant and useful for those who are already leading an organisation and who want to refresh and further strengthen their skills. Time dulls our edge. We must also never forget that sales is the foundation of all business. The book will also be very helpful to entrepreneurs and to those who are moving up the ladder and looking for ways to simplify, improve and increase their impact on their organisation.

In light of the major business and societal changes which we are all currently experiencing, I have ensured that the advice in the book fits our 'new world'. I have also included a final appendix (appendix 4) with my thoughts on business, leadership and Covid-19.

The format follows the same very simple approach that was received so well in my first book. Short chapters, each dedicated to a specific subject with easy, but powerful learning contained in each. It also uses the same 'conversational' tone that so many have commented on.

As in 'The B2B Selling Guidebook' all of the stories in this book are real, BUT have been heavily anonymised.

I have experienced both the highs and lows of being the head of an organisation. Until you have done it, particularly if the organisation is large and complex, you cannot understand the pressures and issues that will hit your desk, day after day. Again, there are too many mentors, examples, competitors and friends to name individually but, as you read the stories, you may well see yourself in there - again! And again, I thank you all for the lifetime of experience – both good and bad – that has enabled me to deliver this second book. 43+ years is a very long time so where I have remembered something incorrectly, please accept my apologies.

"Be the change that you wish to see in the world..."
Mahatma Gandhi

The B2B Leaders Guidebook

A guide to Sales Management
and Business Leadership in the
Real World of Complex Business

Jim Irving
2020

Contents

Section 3. Improving... **165**

Section

1

Starting...

Chapter

1

Introduction

"Two roads diverged in a wood, and I – I took the one less travelled by, and that has made all the difference..."

Robert Frost

As I write this book, I am trying to imagine you, and your situation.

Perhaps you are a salesperson who has just been promoted. All too often it is assumed that a great salesperson also makes a great Sales Manager. Trust me, the skills are very different. Perhaps you have left academia, or have just had a great idea based on your life experience and you are now an entrepreneur running your first start-up business with all of the challenges that poses... and there are so many facing the first-time business creator. Maybe you are in a corporate organisation and have been transferred or promoted to run a team or division. That can be so difficult too. Or you could be an experienced individual running an SME (Small to Medium Enterprise) who wants to upgrade their skills.

This book is for all of you! It's also for anyone who wants to understand the more general dynamics of leading teams in high stress environments, building a business or the world of sales and business leadership.

Just how long have I been involved in teams? Well, the picture below shows me in one of my earlier team environments. This school team was actually well coached and led and very successful in its geography and time... (And my name is misspelt! ☺)

George Dougall   Alec Bull   Jim Irvine
Paul Mowat   Ronnie Cummings   Davie Duthie

Lawrence Chalmers Mickey Stuart   Ian Turton   Alan Hewat   Davie Kellock

Football Team - 1967

What's the situation today as I write, just 'a few' years after that picture was taken? I am sitting at home, as I have been for many weeks now during the 2020 Covid-19 lockdown. The perfect time to start work on a large project!

This is my second book. The first, 'The B2B Selling Guidebook', was very successful in its own right and also opened up a number of new business and personal connections for me. While writing the draft of that book I realised that I hadn't even covered half of the experiences and learning I wanted to share. So, I altered the planned contents of 'The B2B Selling Guidebook' and then opened out the journey to reflect more of my management and leadership experiences, thoughts and advice in this, second, book.

The approach is the same. This is a light, easy to read, book. It is full of anecdotes and proof points. It is short and to the point – we are all busy and I don't know about you, but I hate lengthy, dry tomes. While some of the content is sales management based, most of the principles and ideas relate to team leadership more generally. Some content from the first book is referenced. But why do I believe I have something more worth sharing? Three things... First, the great response to 'The B2B Selling Guidebook' and its style and approach. There is a need out there. Second, when I added up all my years in leading small teams, branch operations, regional functions, international corporate subsidiaries and then start-ups, I came to a total of 20+ years of front-line, high pressure business management experience. Over dozens of countries, differing markets, multiple organisation types, leading sales only teams, sales and marketing teams and also total company/business operation leadership. Third, I want to make your life easier. In the first book, I mentioned that I had made many mistakes over the years. The same applies to my time spent managing small, medium and large teams and organisations. In fact, I am still learning. But I just make fewer mistakes these days! This book will help you avoid pitfalls and errors, and succeed more quickly.

The book is structured into three phases or sections. First, 'Starting', second, 'Building' and last, 'Improving'. It's possible that you might feel, after reading, that some chapters should be placed earlier in these phases, or later. I struggled with categorising some of them myself. But the actions and skills are in – roughly – the right order for most situations.

So, let's travel together through the steps to great leadership and career success together...

The Lesson
Forget what you already 'know' and join me in looking afresh at different ways to achieve greatness.

"An expert is someone who knows some of the worst mistakes that can be made in his subject, and how to avoid them."

Werner Heisenberg

Notes

_____

_____

_____

_____

_____

_____

_____

_____

_____

_____

_____

_____

_____

_____

_____

_____

_____

_____

_____

_____

_____

_____

_____

_____

Chapter

2

It's the Hardest Job – Really!

"The real challenge is to combine strong leadership and strong management and use each to balance each other."

Philip Kotler

I hate to be the bearer of bad tidings but...

All business/business psychology theory seems to agree on one point. Of all the roles in an organisation, the 'worst and most stressful' is that of the 'First or 'Front' Line Manager'. Why?

Think of your own organisation. The 'workers' just, well... work. Those layers (sometimes only one above, at worst up to five or so on top) of managers and directors/owners tell them what to do and their job is to just get on and do it. For better or worse. Maybe hard work, but simple. Those who run the Division, or business, overall, are required to manage and to lead. Their entire focus is on doing just that. Their life, in relative terms, is also simple and focussed. Only at one level does someone have to try and work with – and please – both upper management AND 'the workers' simultaneously. The first line manager role involves more conflict and stress, trying to help both sides of the business organisation equation at the same time, than the other two combined. This is, of course, also magnified where this is a unionised environment and that potential conflict is added to the mix as well. Three different vectors then collide right on top of the first line manager.

Just step back and think of it. Let's say you are a first line manager or team leader. The Director says something has to be done. You say *"yes"*. Even as you leave the meeting or finish the conference call, you already know that your team will hate it. Bang! No one else is conflicted but you are already, and the conflict hasn't even started yet!

Ah, *"but it's not that difficult for me"* you say. *"I am but a lowly SME business owner"*. Or *"I have a small start-up, it's actually quite simple for me..."*. Let me assure you, if you are saying that, then you have only just arrived in that position and don't understand! Why am I so confident?

Let's take the start-up scenario. You had the idea, started the business and now employ maybe 5-10 people. What do you do, day-to-day? You are responsible for the strategy... and execution... and all business functions... and revenues... and cash... and... well, you get the picture. BUT at the same time, you are also the first line manager for your one or two sales heads too – as well as every other function! (Quite likely having never managed or experienced sales before as well). You have the most conflicted job, PLUS all the higher-level work and pressures too. At least in a larger organisation you only have the first line conflict to cope with.

Surely, we must have arrived at the worst possible scenario, haven't we? Oh, no, not quite. Think of who you manage and have any challenges or conflict with. From all of my years of experience, which function in an organisation is hardest to manage? Sales, every time. Recruited to be creative and frequently outspoken. Confident in themselves, haters of all forms of structure and paperwork. Always knowing the best way for something to be done. Hating close supervision. Oh, and able to argue about anything until you run out of time. I wouldn't mind betting that anyone reading this who has managed a sales team is probably laughing – or at least smiling - right now... (And I write all of the above as a confirmed life-long salesperson!)

Yes, becoming the first-time manager of sales people is the true business 'ultimate challenge'. But any first management role is a difficult step up. And so are all the steps that follow. This book has been written to help you manage the process, avoid mistakes - or missteps if you prefer - and create a team that delivers and exceeds, no matter the function you work in.

The Lesson
In managing a small business, start-up or business unit, be prepared for challenges and complexity. It's your job to lead and to simplify. When you get it right, it's SO good...

"When faced with a challenge, look for a way, not a way out."

David L Weatherford

Notes

_____

_____

_____

_____

_____

_____

_____

_____

_____

_____

_____

_____

_____

_____

_____

_____

_____

_____

_____

_____

_____

_____

_____

Chapter

3

You Only Get One Chance to Make a First Impression

"Go out of your way to make an outstanding first impression."

Robert Cheeke

Before we delve into the details on this subject, and for some light relief, while doing my research I found one of my early payslips. Complete with my name, again misspelt – a bane of my working life to this day. And yes, that was £9.83 for a full week's work!

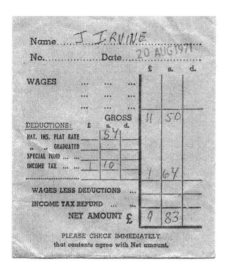

Back to business. The chapter title reflects a well-known truism. You really do only get that one chance to make a - hopefully, good - first impression. What on earth does that have to do with sales or indeed, any other type of leadership? How does it apply as you go up the ladder in your career? How powerful is the effect of making a strong first impression with a new team or organisation?

That first impression in business is all important. The people in the team or division, or company are watching and waiting to see what you are like. So, do try to make a positive impact. It's difficult to quickly recover from a poor start. Let me give you an example or two. Several come to my mind immediately...

Let's start from the perspective of you being new 'in post' in an established organisation. Many times in my career I have been in this position with a team just waiting to see what I was like. Each time I wanted to prove that I was both open and different...

One thing I have learned over my career is that there is always a right and a wrong time to do things. Let's assume you have just found out are the winning candidate. It could be an external selection, or internal, it makes no difference. Before you even meet the team; at that moment when the decision is made – before you are even announced to them – start to plan on creating a strong first impression on them and making an immediate impact. Two examples of this follow for you to consider, but there could be more when you start to think of how you can maximise this point in time. You are literally at the point of 'maximum leverage' in that *"we want you"* job conversation with a new employer or Director. You will not have that same level of power in a month's time. So, use this time wisely. Before we dig into my own thoughts on this subject, here's an associated tip for you to use to your own benefit. A mentor of mine gave me this advice... *"When your potential new employers have decided they want you, take a minute and then insist, as part of your package, on an extended leaving arrangement"*. I was confused and he then explained. *"As they hire or appoint you, they are not thinking of the long-term future. It's a complete 'non item'. If the norm is, say, a month's notice, insist on 3 months. If 3 months, then insist on 6 months"*. Every time I have done this in my career since, there has been a shrug of the shoulders and agreement. Those on the other side of the table want to clear off the obstacles to you taking up the post. Then, when a number of years have passed and it's time to leave, you have that extended time you negotiated at the start, to work with. Just a thought...

But, of course, the idea I suggest above is entirely self-serving. So, in that same conversation with those who are recruiting me, I also ask for the ability and/or the authority and/or the budget to sort a current problem. In effect to have, in your back pocket, a hunting licence to make an impact by delivering a 'win' for those who will work for you. I have done this several times and it really makes a positive impact and, at the same time, it sets your position as the leader. To be clear, this is not a bribe or anything like it. Be careful not just to play a game. What you are actually saying if you do this, is *"give me the ability to make an early, highly positive impact on the team to prove I will always think of them"*. I will give you several clear examples of this technique in real-life action in the next chapter...

In two cases, when pointed to my corner office on the first day, or in one case asked where I wanted it to be after an office refurbishment, I rejected the idea itself. *"Put the office where you want, but make it into a meeting room. Give me a desk in the centre of the open plan office"*. Now, this may not always be the right thing in every single situation, I accept that. You might not be used to such an idea. It might be a giant step out of your comfort zone. Your team may work on highly confidential items and I can understand that. From my experience though, doing this can send a strong message. With a bit of research, you can establish what impact that announcement might have. For me, each time it did send a very strong message – 'open attitude', 'part of the team', 'no closed doors', 'different' etc. I still had a meeting room available for when I had to action things privately. But in the main, sitting inside the team area created a totally different environment and atmosphere. Of course, things were overly quiet and stilted at first ☺, but as people relaxed it became the new norm. Boy, did I hear how people really worked, what time they arrived in and left, interacted and focussed - or didn't. With this working approach, of course, you need to ensure that the team are reminded from time to time that you are the leader. It's really OK to be relaxed and informal, it's absolutely not OK to revert back to just being a team member.

So far, these initial thoughts have been about you joining an organisation – or being promoted. What if it's your own organisation? Let's now assume you have just created a start-up or have got past that stage and are running your own functioning SME. What then? Here it is simple, you OWN the culture, attitude and atmosphere in your company. If you start off bullying and shouting then, guess what? That will become the standard, accepted culture as the business grows. (I have visited the branch operations of partner companies and seen behaviour that EXACTLY mirrored the founder's personal attitudes, shouted outbursts and personality. That didn't happen by accident). If you never set goals for targets to be achieved, then that will be the internal norm. If missing targets or objectives is OK and then never mentioned again, the same applies. While it's best to think about your company right at the start, it is never too late to take time to define how your team should operate, the basics, the standards, the expectations and ethical rules that you set. Even if you have been there for years, take time now and think about what is right and expected. This book will not address the 'how'. You can have a mission or vision statement, and/or a 'we believe' type list of values. There are many approaches. The point is this, take the time to decide how you want your business to operate. What are your ambitions and objectives, what behaviour towards each other and your customers is acceptable or not? Lay those thoughts out clearly, in some way, then LIVE by them. So many organisations have these statements and they only actually live on the website or the notice board. They have no value or purpose. It has to be real – and actively used and enforced – to be effective. It's worth a good bit of your time to set it out both to reflect your desires and 'the rules'. Make it visible and actually followed.

You have now set your company up or you have set your start date in your new role. What do you do as you arrive to start work, on that first day?

Think VERY carefully about your first comments to the team. How do you want to appear? What are the core three things you want them to take away from that first session? How do you prove your credentials without seeming boastful? On that front, I typically asked the person introducing me before we went in, to talk to the team about my relevant experience and achievements. That, of course, explains why you were appointed and also means you don't have to say the words yourself! Then clearly lay out the messages you want to deliver. Again, I tended to cover roughly the following – *"Here is where we are as a team"* (relating to their previous and current performance), *"here is how I work"* to let them know up front my approach and give an example of what is good in my opinion and what is bad. For example, *"I expect you to take reasonable risks and try new ideas. That's a good thing to do. If you are worried about how to do something, then just come to me, I will never criticise your requests for help. But if you do take a risk and it fails – and could impact the company - tell me. If you do, then we will learn together from it and I will back you, if you don't and I hear after the fact please be assured, I will not be happy"*. In doing this you have explained how they should conduct themselves and how you will respond to two very different responses, while starting to lay out the rules. Those are just examples of what I said. What would be right for you? What would be your core messages? Everyone approaches this differently – but just THINK about it beforehand. No preparation is a recipe for a poor first impression.

If you hadn't thought about doing any of this and your company/team is already established and just 'working away' you haven't lost the opportunity. Call a team or company meeting, explain that you are remiss in never having done this before and then lay out your '5 core values', 'Goals for the year', 'Do's and Don'ts' or whatever is appropriate to you and your situation. One of the first keys to consistent team or company success is having everyone understand the goals, the rules of engagement and the standards that are expected. If you don't start with clear objectives you are half way to losing before you begin.

In my own career I have seen salespeople promoted who then carried on exactly as before. But of course, now they were the manager – so there was nothing to stop them doing their own thing, as they had always done in selling. No team coaching, mentoring, support or leadership. The result? Mayhem, arguments, no team identity, membership or shared goals at all...

Finally, do take some time to consider what type of organisation you are working for. This might be obvious, but in my experience almost no one does it. What exactly do I mean by this? First, I hope as a leader you actually don't have to make the choice that follows and can always manage to create or work in a truly 'balanced' or measured company, but in my experience these beasts are rare. Why? At their absolute core every organisation has what I call its 'Ultimate, Dominant Gene', or UDG for short. This is the UDG you create as a founder, or it is the one that an existing company (often unconsciously) works to. Business, economic and management theory talks about this under various guises, but let me cut all the academic stuff down to just this paragraph. There are only so many routes that a company can – when backs are to the wall and push comes to shove – use as their core, fundamental guiding – and overriding principle –

- **Finance led.** After everything else is considered, is it the finance department (or your external VC (Venture Capital) or angel investors) that make the final strategic decision, based on those financial numbers?

- **Engineering led.** Often, especially in Tech companies, the engineers/developers have the power and final say

- **Manufacturing led.** Less common these days. But in the large-scale manufacturing environment this can be the #1 power base. *"What will manufacturing say?"*

- **Market led.** These companies always revert to following, or trying to lead, the market they already operate in

- **Marketing led.** In some cases, companies rely on marketing to make those final decisions. Where to focus, what to change etc

- **Sales led.** I have worked in several of these. Whatever happens, the business must do what sales says it needs.

- **The cult of the leader.** In a number of technology companies I have seen, it was/is the founder or leader who 'knows and decides' everything. Argument and discussion are futile. Just keep your head down and do what is demanded. This is, of course, inefficient and liable to lead to major strategic decisions going badly, but it is all too common.

Just look at this list a minute. If you are to be successful internally, how would your own strategy for your team differ if you worked in each of these environments? How would you approach big problems? Where, if you have to get political support, do you go? Or, if you are in a start-up, which of these is the right way for you to go, for the long term? They are all important, but you really can only have one UDG. What is (or should be) yours?

Anyway, you have made your first comments and everyone goes back to their desks and work recommences. What do you now do over the first couple of weeks in post?

The Lesson
Focus very carefully on that first impression. Set clear and simple expectations. If you are already up and running, take the time out to set – or reset – your vision and standards. And don't forget your organisation's UDG!

"Almost everyone will make a good first impression, but only a few will make a good lasting impression."

Sonya Parker

Notes

Chapter

4

Your First Actions

"An idea not coupled with action will never get any bigger than the brain cell it occupied."

Arnold Glasow

Those first two to three weeks are critical in getting the team behind you, in building energy and momentum and creating a trusting and positive environment. But how, exactly, do you get things moving? Through trial and error, nothing more scientific than that, I have found a recipe to get things moving positively. If you want to sit behind a desk and 'manage' then this process is not for you. This is hard work.

You need to be prepared and ready to build on the first impressions and create real momentum. The following picture is one of my all-time favourites. Its source is long lost in the mists of time. But I have been at this 'starting out afresh' stage a number of times and this is usually how I feel! You think you are prepared; you are ready, technically 'properly equipped' and fully set up to move fast – but you just know things could go very wrong! The picture still makes me smile.

Proper planning and thought beforehand means you should never be quite so exposed as in the picture. BUT, it's a critical time for you and for your new team.

Remember, you have already 'banked' an ability to solve something for the team. And you need to get to know them. Here's what I did first. I announced that I wanted to get to know everyone at a personal level. I then organised a 20-minute, private chat with everyone in the team. Easy when I did it with a team of eight, but a real commitment when it's not far under 90! But I did just that – and have done so a number of times now. If you have reached the apex of your career to date and have hundreds or thousands of people 'below' you, then just make sure you do this for your direct reports, perhaps to two or three levels below and a sample of the others too. You can always do another one or two each time you visit a geography, a branch or team. What did I discuss when I did it? Here are my bullet points...

- *"What is your role and how long have you been doing that?*

- *Give me a rough understanding of your career to date?*

- *What do you enjoy in your role and what do you dislike?*

- *Where do you want to be in a couple of years?*

- *What skills do you need but don't have yet?*

- *Tell me about yourself outside work? Family, interests etc*

- *Now, tell me the 3 things you think are most broken, annoying to you, about your employment here right now? I don't promise I can do anything but I will consider them all. And no prizes or penalties for what you say – be honest..."*

- (All of the above was kept entirely confidential by me. And each person knew it would be)

Guess what? Every time, I got to know the person quickly. Equally important, I understood how they fitted into the organisation, and as importantly I knew their 'complaints' and concerns. Almost everyone I have done this with was, I think, pretty honest. They appreciated the approach and interest. I very quickly understood the current dynamics inside the team/company. I heard of things I could fix quickly for individuals – and I then made sure I fixed them. I also then instantly – in all three cases – saw perhaps two or three areas that EVERYONE across the team was concerned about. And that's where I called on my 'banked' favour - held ready for me to use, by those above me. Each time I explained and asked for their agreement, management said 'yes' and I was then able to solve at least one of those big, shared problems. But I was also now aware of those others that I could work on in the short to medium term as well. They became a focus for me in my role. In one case their big issue was actually under my control to amend anyway. What sort of things are we talking about?

- The team targets (in this case, for a sales team) had been ramped up massively by a previous director, now long gone. It was obvious they wouldn't achieve them, no matter what they did. Result? Dreadful morale. I negotiated an agreed reduction in their targets. Not to a level they were happy with (what sales person is ever happy with their target!?) but to one they could understand and strive to achieve. This wasn't a weak team complaining, this was a stratospheric and completely unrealistic goal they all knew (as did senior management, as it turned out) was impossible to achieve.

- The company pension scheme – made up of three options, had adopted 'average to poor' investment offerings for the team. These were now 'fixed' and immovable. 'Always been there and can't change'. A single two-hour meeting with the company external

Pensions Advisor generated another, much better rated pension option to add to the existing options. At no extra cost...

· Specific aspects of the working terms and conditions were way below market par. A bit of research and a meeting with the HR Director enabled me to change several of them for the better.

What impact do you think these almost immediate outcomes would have on a team? I have been open... I have proved my interest by spending personal time with them.... I have taken on board their common concerns (and along the way fixed things for a few individuals) and improved at least one of their overall biggest issues... How do you think they responded when I started to lay out what I had as my vision and goal for the team? With their arms folded or with an open attitude? The basis of trust had been achieved within around two weeks total.

But these are just my ideas. No matter what situation and position you hold (or are about to inhabit), think about how you can get the team behind you. Do you think you would do better shouting from behind a desk? Or does this personal, interested and committed approach promise much more? Well, in <u>every</u> case this worked both for me and for the team. No theory here, just my gut instinct on what would get everyone the right result quicker. Of course, this then has to be part of your inner attitude. You can't do all of this, then sit behind the desk and shout! It's not a trick, it's a permanent way of thinking.

Oh, and by the way, are you more or less likely to understand someone who is differing or arguing with you when you already know what makes them tick and how they view the world? No brainer...

The Lesson
Take time to listen to your new team. You simply cannot lead people you don't know. Do SOMETHING positive quickly.

"People may doubt what you say, but they will believe what you do."

Lewis Cass

Notes

_____

_____

_____

_____

_____

_____

_____

_____

_____

_____

_____

_____

_____

_____

_____

_____

_____

_____

_____

_____

_____

_____

_____

_____

Chapter

5

Management -v- Leadership

"Management is doing things right; leadership is doing the right things."

Peter Drucker

Are you a manager or a leader? Or are you both? Can you even be both? These are fundamental questions you need to be able to answer as you move up the organisational ladder.

In the business world, these two descriptions are used frequently and often interchangeably. A bit like *"sales and marketing are pretty much the same, aren't they?"* A fair proportion of people might think they are the same but, boy, they are not. And it's exactly the same with management and leadership. What separates them?

A wise old mentor of mine, as he was promoting me to into my most senior role of my career, talked about this subject. *"There is a big difference between the two roles and you have to realise it. There are X,000 people in the organisation and many of them are managers, good managers. Think of our marketplace out there – and our company - as a large field covered in two storey buildings with no doors. Those managers work together every day, in whatever area they manage to ensure the ladders are put up against the walls safely. They make sure the tools are available to gain entry. They ensure their teams are properly trained to go into that building – whatever each one might represent in terms of internal tasks or external projects. They manage all the daily business processes. My job as their leader is simply to ensure the right ladders are placed up against the right buildings..."*

What did he mean? Managers are responsible for processes, procedures, the day to day tactical actions. Leaders take the strategic decisions and should constantly be checking the direction of travel, progress, the landscape and priorities – so that the managers can then execute against the ever-changing world the organisation lives in. This applies equally to internal processes as well as the more obvious external world. It's a lesson I have never forgotten. Have a look in chapter 24 for another idea on strategic thinking and true leadership.

In war, do people charge in to follow their manager? I think not. Where that does happen, we know it often goes very wrong. Leaders excite, exhort, and set the vision – and then lead! They operate and direct at the strategic level. In football or soccer if you will, you can always see the difference between a technically competent captain and a competent captain who is also a true leader. One takes the right steps 'by the book', the other somehow gets even more from his/her teammates on top of the basics and motivates them towards greater success.

Another point and an old bugbear of mine. It is said that managers manage people, right? Wrong. You can manage for the actions and outcomes you want from people but do you actually manage people? When was the last time you managed your spouse or sibling? You are working with, mentoring, disciplining and supporting your team members, but I just don't think you actually manage people...

Which should you be? Leader or Manager? In the real world these are two different skills, but the great manager/leader can do both well. Both the process and the vision. Often, you have no choice. In the SME or start-up environment you are saddled with both.

Let's say you turn out to be a great leader. Well, that's good isn't it? But if you are running a small business and can't do any of the tactical stuff, will it end well? Of course not. The actual work of running the business will become unstructured and fragmented. Similarly, if you can administer with the very best of them, but can't lead – in any way – will the team stretch and over achieve? Again, we all know the answer.

Now, everyone tends to lean naturally to one or other of these ends of the spectrum. The first step is to take some time, be humble and realistic with yourself, look honestly at your past, your experience, what others say about you and which of these roles you are most comfortable in. THEN consciously focus on doing more in the other area. Step out of your comfort zone and work to become equally good (or at least, a good bit better), in your weaker area. Those who get to the top are often able to step between both roles as needed. The mentor I mentioned above had fantastic strategic vision and capability AND was the most detailed micro-manager when it was required. I would suggest that none (or very few) of us are born with both of these attributes ready baked. We will come more naturally to one and have to work at the other. Knowing where you sit today is the start of your journey.

If you now look back at the previous chapter and my approach to the first couple of weeks in a new role, you will see a mixture of management process and strategic thinking in play...

The Lesson
Where, when and how should you manage? Where, when and how should you lead? If you don't already know the answer – or the difference, then find out!

"Be not afraid of growing slowly, be afraid only of standing still."

Chinese Proverb

Notes

_____

_____

_____

_____

_____

_____

_____

_____

_____

_____

_____

_____

_____

_____

_____

_____

_____

_____

_____

_____

_____

_____

Chapter

6

Turn Their World Upside Down!

"In order to be irreplaceable,
one must always be different."

Coco Chanel

What a strange chapter title. Does this refer to a fiendish new management theory? Not at all. I actually mean what the title says!

Everyone in the working world knows the organisation chart. 'The Pyramid.' Serfs at the bottom, the big cheese at the top. It's my belief that this is an entirely incorrect view of the world of work today. First of all, who do we all say is the most important person to the organisation? It's the customer of course. So where are they on the organisation chart? Nowhere. It's not such a crazy idea to include them...

Look at the 'normal' organisation chart below (one I took at random from google for a large company – one of hundreds of millions out there).

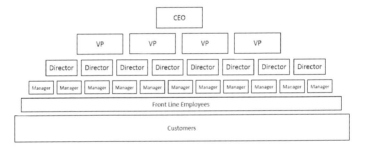

All pretty standard. Who is the most important person here? It's pretty obvious. But this example is actually far better than most because at least it includes the customer, but the customer is at the bottom of the chart – and therefore subliminally - the least important.

Now let's take that same org chart and flip it.

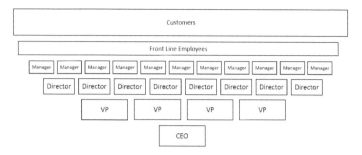

Or, pictured more simply for any sized organisation –

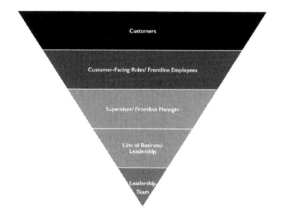

In terms of the image you want to portray both internally and to the outside world, how do the second and third ones compare with a typical organisation chart? First, the most important 'person' is now the customer. In second place, it's those who support and interact with the customer. And the big cheese? His/her job (and his/her direct reports) is to support everyone who engages with the customer and the customer themselves. You have just reset the whole perspective internally and externally for your organisation.

And yes, this does work equally well when you move to smaller organisations. I have introduced this model into a number of organisations and each time there has been a mindset change. IF you then live by it. As well as your internal role as leader of the team or business, you are now also identified in the org chart as the person who has the job of supporting team members and customers. It's a great visual image. But even more, it also goes down fantastically well with prospective customers as you present your company and offerings to them. In fact, I have not only had a 100% positive experience using this type of slide, I have actually had a large number of senior executives from the customer organisation asking for that slide and where to get working copies so they can then apply it to their organisation.

Simple!

The Lesson
Think differently, act differently, deliver value and change from Day One. And why not turn their world upside down while you are doing it! Try it just once, you will never look back.

"You're either part of the problem or part of the solution."

Eldridge Cleaver

Notes

Chapter

7

Creating Team Identity

*"Coming together is a beginning.
Keeping together is progress.
Working together is success."*

Henry Ford

The creation of a team identity and the supporting values is in my view a good thing to do as early as you can. But what actual steps can you take to achieve your goals in this regard?

In this area of work there is a lot of science. I have tried quite a few things over the years. There are many theories out there. Do they work? Who knows! But here is what has worked for me.

1. Be open. From the outset, don't think 'them and us' or 'them and me'. Assume that most team members will want to work together and better. So, where you can, always be open and clear.

2. NEVER use 'you' when talking about your team members, it must always be 'we'.

3. If you can, and if it's appropriate, create a team name or 'branding' even within a larger organisation. Use colour, what is put up on the walls, a catch phrase – whatever works, to create that sense of unity, identity and difference to the rest of the world

4. Have a vision that you share, coach and lead your team in. If someone asks any one of them *"what makes your team different? What are you trying to achieve?"* what do you think they will answer? If they all say the same thing, you have fully and effectively communicated the vision.

5. Make teams meetings both fun AND clearly defined. ALWAYS use an agenda defining what is to be covered, combined with timings. Do not tolerate lateness, create a sense that they must be there on time. One manager I worked for locked the meeting room door at start time! A bit harsh, well yes, but not as harsh as... another manager removed all the chairs to ensure no one could relax and then set very tight

timings for the session! I have had a (by rotation) 5 question quiz to start, a fun fact or bad news about a competitor's business. In reality the possibilities are endless but they did help to make those sessions effective for the both business and team bonding.

6. Protect your team ferociously when attacked. They will find out and be appreciative (see also chapter 9)

7. Create rituals that everyone enjoys. Two examples. I have – a number of times – gone out on a hot day and bought ice lollies for everyone in the team and dished them out. In one company, a 'Mr Whippy' ice cream van would come to the street outside from time to time. I would head out, put the ice cream equivalent of 'money behind the bar' in a pub and invite everyone who wanted one to come and get them. I have also used my discretionary budget (read my first book for far more on that subject) to create spot team prizes – rewards and awards – given out to those who had gone above and beyond. In doing this I included and recognised everyone, not just sales people.

8. As early as you can, give your team an activity or project to work on. *"I see that we are always losing to Acme Inc. I want all eight of you to split into sets of two and come back to the team in five days with two ideas from each team to improve our win rate against them"*. (Optionally followed by "and the ideas I believe to be best win a prize".)

9. Celebrate! Always find a ritual to celebrate the really big achievement. In selling, I have seen a bell rung by the person who has closed a really big deal. I have seen a flashing light lit up too. If it's a team effort then, if your budget allows, take them out. But whatever you do, do something! Buy cakes, anything. I have experienced the opposite and it's the world's worst feeling...

10. Delegate whenever you can. It is important to show you trust team members, to give them a chance to develop and to improve their skillset. There is a great by-product of this, you have more time to plan to lead and to review when you have delegated. But get the balance right – never too much. Do it for everything and your team will start to believe (probably rightly) that you are lazy, not actually delegating for a positive reason.

Many, many years ago I was working for a large corporate. I was near to closing a very big deal in a vertical marketplace – let's call it market 'X'. My immediate boss, a charismatic and well-liked boss was replaced by a 'manager'. The new manager called me in. *"I want you to focus on market 'Z' from now on"*. Just a short while later that big deal did come in and I was over the moon. A year's work had come good. The revenues and profits for the company were substantial. I arrived back at the office with the order and my colleagues all congratulated me but the manager's door remained closed. I went for lunch and on my return, I saw an envelope sitting on my keyboard. The manager's door was closed again. I opened up the envelope and a memo was inside, I can still remember the words, well over 25 years later – *"Jim, I note that you have sold to Smith and Co who are not a 'Z'"*. Signed...

That was it. Not only no recognition, praise or reward, but a formal, negative comment on something that they disapproved of, entirely without any context. How did I feel? I think anyone reading this could imagine. I left soon after and, working for a major competitor, made it my mission in life to (very successfully and profitably ☺) lead a team that took multiple large deals away from my old employer. Looking back now, with my life experience, I still get angry thinking of that response. Now imagine if that manager had come out, joined in the congratulations and then said (privately) something like *"Very well done Jim. That was a great deal! Now, how can we work together to do the same in our new target marketplace..."* What a difference a minute's thought (or lack of it) can make, in this case to my career and to two competing businesses. Also, in retrospect, that move I made laid the foundation for all the career success that followed for me! But I learned from that incident and vowed never to be like that as a leader.

The Lesson
Think about your team. It's your job to create the culture, identity and processes. Plan, lead them AND be positive and spontaneous when something goes well. Never take success, or great effort for granted...

"Talent wins games, but teamwork and intelligence win championships."
Michael Jordan

Notes

_____

_____

_____

_____

_____

_____

_____

_____

_____

_____

_____

_____

_____

_____

_____

_____

_____

_____

_____

_____

_____

_____

Chapter

8

It's YOUR Business

"Responsibility equals accountability equals ownership. And a sense of ownership is the most powerful weapon a team or organisation can have."

Pat Summitt

One day we are given our first management role and responsibility say, as a sales, marketing or customer service first line manager. The immediate temptation is to simply ask what your specific, direct goals are and focus on them alone and entirely. Most do just that.

The same applies if you are running a division of a large corporation. Those measures can be simply too tightly defined. For example, for many years in sales I was tasked with a simple revenue target. But, ask any start-up or perhaps a 'reseller' leader - those organisations who buy from a manufacturer in any market and then resell those products, usually with some 'Value Added' – hence VAR - what is important and they will say, profit, cash and only then revenues. Never 'just revenues.' After all, your company could sell £10m of solutions and 'only' make 1p in every £ loss – ending up with an overall loss of £100K! If you only had a revenue target you wouldn't even realise there was a problem *"We sold £10m – fantastic news!"*.

How do you get around this issue? Well, it's really simple. In all the roles I took on in the second half of my career I insisted that my team, branch, division or country subsidiary reports showed that entity as an independent business. This quickly taught me a number of things...

1. More revenue is good, but NOT if it is unprofitable revenue.

2. Gross Profit (your total revenues less the direct cost of generating those revenues) is a better measure of actual performance. Again, you could have high revenues, but even higher costs to get there. Not good...

3. Net Profit (your total revenues, less all the direct costs to generate them and also minus all the 'indirect' costs – or overheads – your company incurs to get you there. Marketing, HR, administration, buildings,

power, insurance etc.) is a far better true measure of relative performance. If you are not directly responsible for generating revenue at least you can see what your true cost to the organisation is, in return for the services you provide.

4. Cash truly is king. You can only go for so long asking your bank to help. If, on average, each month, there isn't enough cash coming in to support the business costs, you don't really have a business.

Looking at all of these, instead of just a single measure, will massively change your perspective and your usefulness to your team and to the wider business. You have now truly become a Business Leader, not just a Sales, Marketing, Finance or Production Leader. The difference is enormous. Suddenly you want to balance increased costs against what they will deliver. You will understand the need for cash. You will see why net profit is so critical a measure. You will become better at running your own business and/ or a much more powerful and balanced leader of your start-up, team or division inside the broader organisation.

The Lesson
Having this approach to your business responsibilities sets you up for further growth, ever larger career steps and ultimately, greater success. Always look at whatever you are responsible for in this context. Those above you (or in the case of start-ups, perhaps the VC's who are funding you) will have much more respect for the leader who looks at the broader picture and implications for the business. So just do it.

"Everything changes for the better when you take ownership of your own problems."
Robert Ringer

Notes

_____

_____

_____

_____

_____

_____

_____

_____

_____

_____

_____

_____

_____

_____

_____

_____

_____

_____

_____

_____

_____

_____

_____

_____

Section

2

Building...

Chapter

9

The Best Approach?

"*Teamwork is the ability to work together toward a common vision. The ability to direct individual accomplishments toward organizational objectives. It is the fuel that allows common people to attain uncommon results.*"

Sun Tzu

You have your new job, your new team and a set of goals. Before we delve into the detailed actions and ideas to build success, what general approach have I found to be the most effective?

As you will have gathered in chapter four, I am not a believer in the 'just shout louder' school of leadership. Here, in my view, are the things you need to combine and balance in order to succeed long term –

- You have to establish you are the leader of the business or unit. Encourage debate and discussion on subjects but make it clear – and enforce the idea – that when the debate is done and you have decided, that's it. Business life is not a democracy.

- Be with the team, but not an actual team member. It's very easy to slide into just being one of the lads/gals, or the other way around, to try to manage purely by instruction. Both of these approaches work badly – and I know that for a fact! As I said in the introduction, lots of mistakes... ☹

- Bearing in mind the above, do actually be friendly and interested at a personal level. Small talk, as long as it doesn't take up the day, is a good thing. It increases the social connection and sense of sharing and partnership between all parties.

- When there is an issue, defend the individual(s) in any public forum, quietly and professionally. THEN, take them aside and tell them, to their face, never by memo, what you think. But when you do that, again do it professionally and clearly. Use logic and sense, not threats and volume.

- Be – and be seen to be – firm but fair. If you tear down a bit when something bad happens, make sure you equally praise and thank them, when things are done well. All of one, or the other, is a recipe for problems.

Every individual has their own style. So, we will all do the above things in different ways. But let's just make sure that our teams can at least respect and understand us. Above all, think of how you would like to be treated.

The example story below actually comes from my first book. But it bears repeating, by way of an example of almost doing the right thing almost in practice. Looking back, I can see things I would do differently. My first ever sales management appointment was to a branch in very serious trouble. 49th out of 49 in the UK. Deeply in the mire. The story in The B2B Selling Guidebook picks up right there...

I was in before them, away after them and always available to help. I covered their backs with senior management as early forecasts dropped short. Over time we actually became a real team. We won and lost together. We started to want to achieve for each other. This may sound corny, but one of the nicest moments in my 40+ year career was when, after a particularly important month ended with us missing target – yet again – and I had been beaten up by senior management – yet again – we were having a bite of lunch and one of the guys quietly handed me an envelope. I opened it up and it was an apology card signed by everyone in the sales and pre-sales team saying they were really sorry, and it wouldn't happen again. We had bonded, and they felt for my situation and for me. Fast forward nine months and the UK monthly newsletter (which I still have a copy of) had a note from the UK Sales Director saying *"...and finally, could any other branch than X please win the monthly league table, it's getting boring..."* Yes, we had gone from 49th to top. The team was performing...

The Lesson
Think now about how you will start to build the team, what your style will be, how will you react when faced with a challenge or issue, how you will lead, how you will manage. This time investment will pay you back a hundredfold...

"It is the long history of humankind (and animal kind, too) that those who learned to collaborate and improvise most effectively have prevailed."

Charles Darwin

Notes

Chapter

10

Ask Questions!

"A prudent question is one-half of wisdom."

Francis Bacon

"If they can get you asking the wrong questions, they don't have to worry about the answers."

Thomas Pynchon

Questions are pretty well the foundation of everything we do and learn in business. As a manager they become even more important as you work with your team.

Think of a great leader or mentor that has helped you. Did they lecture? Harangue? Or did they observe and ask you questions, then use your replies to help you move forward? For my part, every single one of the (several) great mentors who helped me through my career were able to ask simple questions to get to the core of the matter or problem. Was it uncomfortable? Sometimes it definitely was! Did it open my eyes further each time? Absolutely.

Today, we are literally blessed by our ability to learn simply by 'asking google'. We have more information, research results and advice at our fingertips than every generation of humanity that has gone before us. We have at our fingertips, the vast majority of the written wisdom, experience, theories and approaches across all mankind available on our screen. Just think about that fact for a second... There are too many, for me it's what works in my world that matters most.

I just decided to put 'questioning skills' into google. In 0.44 seconds, it delivered me 84.5 million results! On the first page, some of the most frequently read headings included – 'what are good questioning techniques', 'what are the four (or three, or five, or six, or seven!) types of questions', 'different types of questions', 'questioning skills and techniques', 'effective questioning', 'questions to use in selling', 'questioning skills', 'questioning skills exercise' etc. 84.5 million! You will already have your own learned (from parents, teachers, social life, skills training) approach to questioning. The point is this. However you question today, don't assume that is right, fit for purpose or good enough. Take some time, read, watch and learn online. Tune and improve your questioning skills – to make yourself a more rounded person, to be able to question more effectively and to support your team.

When you talk about questioning as a skill there are almost too many articles and videos as discussed above. But in reality, there really are some fundamentals. Obviously, questions can be closed – they can only be answered 'yes' or 'no', or open – they require explanation, discussion, comment. The difference can be seen between *"did you do..."* or *"can you do x for me today"* (closed) questions and open-ended ones like *"how do you feel about..."* One is yes/no and the other requires thought and discussion/commentary. Both have their uses. To gain commitment or collect specific data, closed questions are better. To dig into something and flesh out more information, for example, the open questions serves far better.

Leading sales trainers and research organisations appear to have also come to an understanding that there are between three and six question types. (have a good look at some of those articles and images as I mentioned above on google). Most of them focus on around four or five. From my own experience and the courses I have attended, I agree with that definition. But do take a bit of time to research a framework you can understand and use, both in your private and business life. Theory is of no use if the model doesn't work for you - but any sensible model will immediately make you better. Here is a way that I think of the different types (other approaches are available!) -

Type 1. Checking questions. These are the basic ones we use to check on anything. Parents know these all too well... *"Have you packed your gym kit?" "What time is the swimming lesson today?"* And in business *"Who will be at today's meeting?"*. Simple and clear. They help you to check the state of things as they are, so you don't suffer from surprises...

Type 2. Questions to find out more/to <u>gather answers on the situation</u>. These are the bread and butter of business, BUT, all too often both salespeople and leaders only skim the surface. What do I mean? Think of a sales meeting which you are leading. So, *"Anne have you made your number this month?" "No". "Ah, OK"*. Now, many immediately ask *"Well, what about next month then?"*. WRONG. These data gathering questions should be much more multi layered. This **first level** is pretty self-evident as just shown. It's all about the facts, the basics.

The next step is the first dig down to the **second level**. Here you are wanting more understanding (and of course this applies equally in all business and personal life conversations and situations). You might say, following on from above *"You must be disappointed with that. What happened?"* Now you are starting a much more focussed conversation, your intent will be to try and uncover the real, underlying problem or issue. Of course, that was an open question and replies in this case might involve things like delays to decisions, lost deals, a new competitor or their belief that the product or service you are selling isn't adequate. The same applies in any other business context. This is never a yes/no dialogue.

You get those answers and you should again go further to the **third level**. This is where the real stuff happens. You have now established the basic facts; you have looked at the problem. The third level takes you into the real implication, end result or consequence. Again, in this manager/salesperson conversation you might say *"I calculate that this takes you to just 60% of your annual target with only 2 months of the financial year left. What's the implication of that for you reaching your annual goals? What can you/we do about it?"* This is the more difficult, but highly rewarding level of discussion. They are now thinking about the situation they are in, how to claw back more business, perhaps even what might happen if they miss their target by a wide margin. It's at this level that you see the real issues, challenges and consequences, NOT that first level many people stop at. In another example situation, say speaking to a customer who has called you in because they have problems with their current solution that you want to replace. Once you have understood those first two levels, then you can say things like *"so what was the consequence of your shut down?" "What was the cost to you of missing the summer market because of the late decisions?" "Did the inability to deliver impact your customers and their perception of you?" "If you add all of those issues together what do you think the total $ cost impact has been to you?"* You are now framing a situation and the value of what you can do to help – weighed against that properly defined problem and the real world consequences to them.

When sitting down with team members, peers or customers always remember those three levels when you are seeking more information. NEVER stop at that first level – it's far too superficial. Going further gets to the real issues and then enables you to understand the true result and inference of the problem – what it really means and then what you can do. These steps are fundamental to the 'value selling' approach to sales. They are also fundamental to running a business or team. How can you ever measure the value you can deliver if you don't know the scale or measure of the problem you can solve?

Some methodologies have been specifically created to address the 'best' approach to questioning. One I was trained in many years ago is 'SPIN' which stands for Situation – Problem – Implication – Need and Payoff. You can see a similar pattern to this approach and it is widely covered and discussed online.

Type 3. Questions addressing how people feel about given subjects. This aspect of questioning is, I find, very often ignored in business. But it's critical. You want to find out not only the facts but the emotions around them. *"How do you feel about our idea?" "Do you think the Board likes our proposal?" "Are you comfortable with these changes?"* Why bother doing it? Simple. People make decisions, or follow your lead not only based on facts but on emotions too. Emotions play a large part in life, why should we ignore them in our working life?

Type 4. Finally, questions to move things forward, to gain agreement. These exist to help make progress. Unlike the other three categories these questions should always be closed. Yes/No. *"So, if we fix the issue on delivery timings will you proceed?" "If I can get my team to work to fix these extra challenges will you deal with the budget issue?" "We have completed the review of your processes; can we now go together to meet your CFO?"* To each of these there are only two possible answers. You either continue forward or you are facing a problem or objection. If the answer is 'no' what should you do then? That's easy, you step back to Type 2, data gathering style questioning to identify the issue and understand what isn't right yet. In selling this question type is closely aligned with 'closing' or getting the final decision. BUT this is also an incredibly useful tool to establish where you are, or what the reality is, in any situation or discipline.

When you meet with a team member to review performance, or to work together on an issue, ask questions first! Then, when you think you have enough information, ask more. Don't just ask about facts, or data. Ask about their thoughts and feelings on the subject too. Always dig deeper. It doesn't have to feel like an interrogation, but it should be in depth. Shallow questions deliver shallow answers.

As a team, business or division leader sometimes people are afraid to open up to you until they get to know you better. Also, the higher up the ladder you climb the further from the grass roots you move – and that can be both concerning and dangerous. So, what could you do on top of the normal meetings, planning sessions, forecast reviews, one-on-ones to keep your finger on the pulse? Here's a tactic that has worked well for me...

In three leadership roles, I opted to run all the required meetings as you would expect. I then introduced something called 'Lunch with Jim'. Once a week, I would ask three or four (<u>absolutely</u> chosen at random) people to join me for sandwiches at lunchtime. I explained that I really did want to know what was worrying or exciting the team. I wanted to know if there were issues brewing. And everything in that session was to be 100% off the record and private – and I kept to that. I explained that we were all adults and that sharing knowledge was a good thing to do. I would start each lunch with an open question as no one ever wanted to be first to speak! *"So, what do you feel about the new software roadmap?" "How are you finding the new flexible working patterns?"*. I would become the devil's advocate and question the sanity of my own decisions sometimes, in front of them. Every time I did this, the first couple of sessions were fairly quiet, but gradually people opened up. They became, lively, VERY interesting and serious conversations on every topic related to the business and working there, that you could imagine. I actually found people dropping hints to get on the next lunch invite – they obviously had something they wanted to share. The by-products were substantial. First, people became more relaxed in putting forward ideas or concerns generally. Second, I gained early warning – for good and bad, of concerns and opportunities as they developed. Third, over time, the skills of all the team members (admin staff, reception, sales, presales, managers, consulting staff) in proposing ideas and delivering/debating the supporting arguments improved – which I believe was a great result for the business overall. It is good to teach your team members to be effective in questioning and digging themselves, whether with their customers or any other contacts.

The Lesson
In summary then, use questions, ask questions, find different ways to engage with your team through questions. Questions deliver knowledge and wisdom to you, don't minimise their value...

"When you are a leader, your job is to have all the questions. You have to be incredibly comfortable looking like the dumbest person in the room. Every conversation you have about a decision, a proposal, or a piece of market information has to be filled with you saying, 'What if?' and 'Why not?' and 'How come?'."

Jack Welch

"Never tell people how to do things. Tell them what to do and they will surprise you with their ingenuity."

George S Patton

Notes

Chapter

11

Are You a Soft Leader?

"In any moment of decision, the best thing you can do is the right thing, the next best thing is the wrong thing, and the worst thing you can do is nothing."

Theodore Roosevelt

The quote at the end of the last article is from Jack Welch (aka 'Neutron Jack') who took GE (General Electric) from a good company to the largest conglomerate on the planet. The other is from General George S Patton. They both gave great quotes! I will use more of them in this chapter...

Some who have read to this point might think I am perhaps a 'soft' leader. Or maybe slow to act or take action. Let me assure you, despite the fact that I like to collaborate and listen, I am neither soft nor slow to act!

Let me give you some background on these two men. Both delivered fantastic quotes and would have been masters of social media if alive today.

1. Jack Welch was the Chairman and CEO of General Electric from 1981 to 2001. When he left GE, he received a severance package of $420m, still the largest such package of all time. Of course, this takes me back to chapter 3 and my thoughts on pre-negotiation as you start in a job – he was obviously a true master of this. My guess is that he negotiated a % of revenues or profits as his leaving payment when he agreed to take on the role – in a company that was really in the doldrums. He then made it into the biggest in the world but still had that % guarantee when he left, well done him! He demanded that GE had to be either #1 or at worst #2 in every single market they operated in. He was ruthless in this strategy. If they were #3, he just left that market and cut the division. His tactics grew the company market value from $12bn to $410bn. He had his critics, a lot of them, but I would suggest he is someone worth listening to...

2. General George S Patton was an incredibly divisive figure. He led the US Third Army in WWII after achieving serious success in WW1. He is the man responsible for turning everything around, against

the odds, to win the famous 'Battle of the Bulge'. Wikipedia tells us *"Patton's colorful image, hard-driving personality and success as a commander were at times overshadowed by his controversial public statements. His philosophy of leading from the front, and his ability to inspire troops with attention-getting, vulgarity-ridden speeches, such as his famous address to the Third Army, but much less so by a sharply divided Allied high command. His emphasis on rapid and aggressive offensive action proved effective, and he was regarded highly by his opponents in the German High Command."* He was also a man for a quote – but perhaps not all printable! He divided opinions at the end of WWII but before history could review his actions, he died after a car crash in Germany in December 1945.

Why do I bring up these two characters? Well, they were both renowned – and respected - for their decision making and ability to just 'get it right'. Here are their two most famous quotes on that subject...

"It is better to act too quickly than it is to wait too long."
Jack Welch

"A good plan violently executed right now is far better than a perfect plan executed next week."
General George S Patton

Jack Welch also later said, in an article something like (paraphrased) *"Looking back I can't think of any situation where waiting longer to take action ever made things better"*. He was re-emphasising his approach again.

Do you see a theme here? Both are renowned for good decision making, but were they soft or slow? They were the very epitome of the exact opposite. But now go back to the end of the last chapter and read that earlier quote from Jack Welch. What he is saying is that he asked lots of questions, gathered all the information he needed, THEN he acted fast and decisively. Patton did the same. Understand then decide. Leaders need to make the difficult decisions and this approach gives a template for how to do it. The decision and action both lie with you. But first, learn, understand, consult, research – then do what you need to do, as fast as you can. Why on earth would you ever wait?

A personal mentor of mine, also renowned for their strategic thinking and decision making also had an interesting approach (layered on top of the concepts above). He was quick to decide and move on issues. But each time, say sitting on his own or consulting with his team about an issue, he would often finish up with a final question. *"And what happens if we do nothing?"* 90% of the time, it was then very obvious we had to act immediately, but just a few times the best action – only once everything was fully researched and known – was to do exactly that, nothing.

In the early stages of my management career I can remember times when I took 'the easy path'. I thought to myself (without any planning, thinking, consulting or research) *"Maybe it will all just work itself out".* I did the childish thing of hoping it would disappear. Well, guess what, each time it just didn't and it was then much harder to fix/unravel later. A very hard lesson I learned – so please don't make the same mistakes in your own career. Just trust my bad experience and miss that stage out...
Learn → Understand → Research more →
Consult → Decide → **ACT FAST**...

The Lesson
Making the hard decisions that affect others can be tough.
But, if you do it right then it does get easier – and your
success rates will increase too. There is a skill to doing this
that has to be learnt. Usually the hard way...

"Indecision IS a decision."

Anonymous

Notes

_____

_____

_____

_____

_____

_____

_____

_____

_____

_____

_____

_____

_____

_____

_____

_____

_____

_____

_____

_____

_____

_____

_____

_____

Chapter

12

People are Still People

"Our most successful leaders are people who put other people first... in the long run, that's exactly what makes them successful."

Blake Roney

In all of this discussion about do's and don'ts we can sometimes forget that we are dealing with real people. Forgetting that fact is simply a bad thing to do. We are working with, leading, helping, selling to... people. This book is all about business and business is people.

What do I mean? Thinking of people as real people can have a real impact. Two examples...

I was selling very high value and complex technology (seven figures minimum). It was the end of a long, competitive campaign. Three vendors were left in the game. The final step was for reference visits to take place to existing customers of this high value technology. To make things simpler, the customer decided to try to run two major visits in one day. One vendor had already done their allocated visit. That left just two of us. My organisation and the other competitor both looked for our best reference accounts for the visits within a geography and we both found them. All good. I actively chose to go second (or, in reality, last of the three. BTW, look at the theory of 'Primacy and Recency' in The B2B Selling Guidebook. It's a powerful piece of psychology that really works). Come the day I was at the agreed meeting point where I was to pick up the customer evaluation team from my competitor. They were over an hour late and stressed. They had been taken to lunch and it seemed for 'some reason' to have overrun. Now standard sales theory would say you should reduce the time your competitor has with the customer and I could clearly see that was what was being done. BUT as people the customer team were concerned about fairness and were upset, not at me, but for me. Nothing was said, but I knew what they were thinking. At decision time the competitor who had overrun their time and was late, was removed from the final competition. Was that the only reason? Of course not, but at a human level was it a factor? What do you think?

In another life, I was leading a professional team bidding to win a lot of business in a major local government organisation. The final presentations were to take most of the day up to, from memory, around 3pm. We manoeuvred ourselves into the last slot again. This time there were a good number of competitors, each pitching to a set time limit. The audience was made up of IT professionals and a committee of the elected officers of the authority. We arrived in good time (four of us) and found we would have to wait almost an hour. What had happened? EVERY vendor, despite warnings, had overrun, in order to displace those that followed. They had all done it. As we sat, I thought about how those who were sitting in that room all day must be feeling by now. I spoke with my colleagues and we agreed to 'stand out'. When called in we quickly set up. I then addressed the audience. I said something like *"Thanks for your time today. And on that note, I know we are running very late because of all the overruns. We appreciate your time and we will not run a minute over. In fact, thinking of how long your day has been, we have decided that we will cut our session short. Instead of an hour, we will be finished in just 40 minutes..."* The reaction in the room was fantastic. Folded arms were uncrossed and bored faces became animated, smiles broke out. We had thought of them as people. 40 minutes later – exactly - we finished and again thanked them for their time. They in turn thanked us profusely and just a few days later we had won the business. Coincidence? I think not.

So, internally and externally, in the middle of everything that's happening, always think of people as people. They have their work and private lives, they have ups and downs, they face their own challenges and pressures.

I have had disruptive team members who when I sat down with them, opened up to major marital problems. Given some time away to try to sort things out, I was rewarded with better attitude, increased effort and loyalty.

When you inherit a team or recruit into that team, take each person at face value. Assume, with the right coaching, they will want to succeed and to act properly. If you find they don't (a very small proportion in my experience), only then is the time to coach aggressively and/or discipline them. Take time to coach them individually (see the next chapter).

This idea can even spill over into your direct family life. My first wife and I had a large family, birthdays were noisy! But we also felt that the individual was important. So, a tradition started. Each birthday involved the usual party etc. But we also then included another day in that week where the whole day was given over to them (until that time when a day with Mum and Dad wasn't cool, of course!) doing whatever they wanted to do. Just the individual and Mum and Dad.

The Lesson
I know it sounds a bit crazy to even have to say this but, remember your colleagues, your team members, the other people in the organisation, your business partners, prospects and customers <u>are all people</u>. Treat them as you would want to be treated. It makes a big difference...

"Everyone you will ever meet knows something you don't."

Bill Nye

Notes

_____

_____

_____

_____

_____

_____

_____

_____

_____

_____

_____

_____

_____

_____

_____

_____

_____

_____

_____

_____

_____

_____

Chapter

13

How to Coach

"The goal of coaching is the goal of good management: to make the most of an organisation's valuable resources."

Harvard Business Review

One of the most powerful ways to build the competence of a team is through continuous, positive coaching.

The business world is full of concepts, ideas and processes around coaching. In this chapter I will combine my own thinking and experience along with a number of inputs from some of the most highly regarded thought leaders on the subject. Specifically, I will include some publicly available thoughts from The Harvard Business Review, Bizlibrary. com, Dummies.com (the providers of the famous 'xxxxx for Dummies' books and yes, there is a Business Coaching blog from them) and Quantum Workplace.com.

Before getting into the meat of this discussion, here is a story from my past, that emphasises a powerful sales message and the potential for good coaching, which I and another professional both missed. You see, coaching opportunities are everywhere. I was the MD of a major multinational's UK operations. I was in early, as usual. The phone rang (no one else was in). I answered and a voice said "can I speak to the MD please?" I answered, "Yes, you already are". They then said "Oh, that's great, I was hoping to speak to you, we are leaders in providing xxxx to your sector." "Great" I replied, "and what is my sector". There was silence for about 5 seconds then they hung up! I was seriously angry. So angry, that at 9am I rang the company back and asked to speak to the sales director. Getting through I retold the story and told him never to have his staff act so unprofessionally again. I heard nothing more. Later, when the day quietened down, I realised that both I and the Sales Director had missed an opportunity. Perhaps I could have coached and given the Sales Director my thoughts on preparation, what works and doesn't work for very senior contacts and how to deliver a value message that could have been passed on to that salesperson? Could the Sales Director also not perhaps have said something like "I am so sorry about this, but rather than just finishing like this, can I ask a question? If I were to coach and support my salesperson and then have them call you again tomorrow would you agree to take the call?". And with decent preparation and a good offer it might have gone very well for them. Both of us completely missed the coaching moment...

So, on to the core of the challenge. My own experience, plus the excellent research and input from all of these sources above, suggests there are some constants to delivering successful coaching. My challenge for you is to have you read all that follows and ask yourself "how many of these do I use today when coaching?".

I have created a list of things for you to consider as you approach improving your coaching skills – or even starting to coach for the first time.

1. Give those who work for and with you, regular (and not just regular once-a-year!) advice, feedback and coaching. Once in a blue moon does not get you results in coaching. I tend towards informal monthly sessions, with more formal measures and coaching every quarter. But this is your choice. Where a lot of support and coaching is needed, do more! If they are flying and getting it right, you can ease off.

2. What sort of person are you dealing with? In my experience there are only three types of people. People who make things happen, people who say "what just happened" and people who don't even know something has happened! (The last group are sometimes referred to, in a derogatory way, as 'Sheeple'). Which category or type is the person sitting in front of you? Obviously, you need to consider, temper and amend your style with each...

3. When you coach, listen to the other person. Don't come into the session already decided on the outcome. When you give your thoughts and advice then take time to seriously listen to their response. Use the questioning skills I laid out in the last chapter to broaden and deepen the conversation.

4. Give good feedback! Coaching is not about you lecturing. Follow the first three steps above, then watch their progress. Comment and feedback frequently.

5. Do it the right way at the right time. If it is a serious subject, make sure the conversation is private, allow enough time and approach it positively. Don't embarrass individuals by berating them about their shortcomings in public. Praise in public, coach and censure in private.

6. Use regularly set up meetings, chance situations and the day to day ups and downs to enable and deliver coaching moments.

7. Be true to the coaching concept. In my career I have tried, sometimes unsuccessfully, to encourage feedback towards me and my own performance. When I have received it, I have always found it to be helpful and taken the thoughts away and considered them seriously. "Am I really pushing Bill too hard?". "Is my input when they are trying to solve problems not always done at the right time?" This is often categorised or described as '360 feedback'. Be open, not defensive. After all, if you can't take advice or input how can you expect them to?

8. Work together to set measurable, achievable goals for the individual to improve. (SMART is a great methodology – look it up)

9. Don't do it for them. If you agree a plan to improve, give them space and time to try to do it for themselves. There is no learning or growth if you keep on just doing it all.

10. There is often some confusion around the difference between Coaching and Mentoring. Mentoring is a very useful and worthwhile activity, but it is a subset of the wider world of coaching. Coaching takes in the broader aspects of leading by example, training, using situations for instant feedback etc.

11. As you coach, there are multiple opportunities to motivate and build up the individual. Take every opportunity. Let them know when they have done something well.

12. Coach all your team members in the questioning skills I covered in chapter 10. Have them be as capable as you are by questioning – their prospects, customers, peers etc.

13. Think of coaching as a great opportunity for career and sometimes life progression as well. An example. A colleague worked for me and was really effective at what they did. We were having a review session and it was going well. I stepped back from the current role and said something like "what skills do you think you are missing today and what impact would learning them deliver to you?" The individual then explained that when they got to the end of their corporate working life, they wanted to help in the family business. To do so they felt that understanding and using Excel could be a really big help to them. As I listened, I realised that using Excel would also be very helpful to the company right now as their role was complex and technical. "What if I gave you the time to attend a full set of Excel training courses? Would that

help?" You can imagine the response. I didn't ever find out if it helped in later life, but those skills helped to make the individual an even more positive and contributing team member.

14. Measure. If coaching towards performance improvement, always ensure you set agreed goals. Monitor their progress and continue to support.

15. Always encourage those you are coaching to come to you with their own ideas about how to solve the challenge or issue first. Sit and listen to their ideas and thought process before you jump in. Maybe they will have the right solutions already!

16. Learn and practice the 'Feedback Sandwich'. This technique is used in every industry and profession and is, simply, the best way to cover and introduce issues. On looking the phrase up on google I got a vast number of hits on the subject and some fantastic images right on the first page. Most seem to involve hamburgers for some bizarre reason. Universities, business owners, CEOs and great sales trainers use this as do the sciences – and all good coaches. Described at its simplest, it is an actual sandwich. Let's say you have a problem with the individual. First make a positive comment or give some positive feedback, and only then start to introduce the issue at hand. Once discussed, finish with more reinforcing or positive feedback – hence the 'sandwich'. Now, there is some debate about how effective this technique is. I found some criticism amongst the first 10 pages of these 176 million articles and posts, but I can say that it has worked well for me in many situations, marketplaces and organisations. It helps to balance and reduce the impact of critical comments you may have to make. Think of your own experiences. What does it feel like when the first words someone says are critical or negative? I often think the whole

concept of 'getting off on the wrong foot' is all about that negative first comment...

17. Finally, consciously look for those who you can bring in to your team to help with coaching, motivation, new ideas. For my part, I have done this for over 30 years now. Someone with a good reputation from another division of your company. Or from the marketplace. I have had customers deliver (sometime very tough, gulp!) feedback on what it was like to engage with my teams, for example. Think outside of the box.

The Lesson
Coaching is a fundamental skill for any leader or manager. It's not an option, nor is it a 'once in a while' thing. By coaching positively and constructively you could have a massive impact on your team – and their individual lives in the future. Hopefully they will remember what you coach but even if they don't at least, as the old saying goes "They may forget what you said, but they will not forget how you made them feel." Make it an important part of your business life. Success in coaching will deliver success in business.

"Coaching is unlocking a person's potential to maximise their growth."

John Whitmore

Notes

_____

_____

_____

_____

_____

_____

_____

_____

_____

_____

_____

_____

_____

_____

_____

_____

_____

_____

_____

_____

_____

_____

_____

_____

Chapter

14 | Recruit the Best

"The key for us, number 1, has always been hiring very smart people."

Bill Gates

"If you think hiring professionals is expensive, try hiring amateurs."

Anonymous

If you are responsible for a team, start up or division you are most likely in charge of your own recruitment too. Take this responsibility seriously. If you aren't responsible, demand that you are! Every organisation rises or falls depending on the quality of the team members. Poor to average solutions, services and products can be market leading if there is a powerful team behind them. The greatest product ever can disappear into obscurity if the team is lacklustre. And it's exactly the same if the team focus is on internal services for the organisation.

Don't compromise, wait till you get the right person. The pain you experience when the quickly recruited head, especially in Sales, turns out to be a very bad fit, is far worse than any delay you might experience! Trust me, it took me several disasters to find that one out.

I believe there are several schools of thought when recruiting. They fall into three rough categories - and this applies to all job areas and disciplines –

1. I want to be able to dominate the team, so I want to recruit people that I know I will be able to control and if needed, manipulate. I want people I can ensure will be subservient

2. I want people a bit like me but not quite as experienced or 'clever'

3. I want the very best. If they are better than me, that's fantastic

Funnily enough, being a great leader doesn't make you a great recruiter. There is definitely a skill to be developed in your personal recruitment actions. Turning again to the above three categories -

1. I have come across many of these people in my career. They have to be the centre of attention, the

best at everything. They MUST have the last word in team discussions. Guess what, their teams, for some bizarre reason, never seem to excel. Just don't ever be that person.

2. I have had a few managers from this category. In fact, a great leader I worked for in a highly professional organisation actually said to me at the end of a long day of interviews before they hired me *"I have your Profiling Survey results back. I think you are perfect, just like me, but not scoring quite so highly on every measure."* I never did find out if he was joking or not, but that attitude is everywhere. This is far better than approach 1, but not the best.

3. Contrast those ideas with probably the best run organisation I ever worked for. In a radio interview the founder was asked how they recruited people. *"I want to step into any team meeting and be the least clever and experienced person there. When that happens, I can explain the issue or subject then leave the team to work on it, knowing they will do a better job than I could".* Brilliant! And guess what? That organisation was dynamic, innovative, fast moving and exceptionally professional. This to me, after 43 years in business, is the only way to go. Work to bring in the absolutely best people you can – and then empower them to use their skills, intelligence and knowledge to your benefit.

What about the selection process itself? We have moved from a world where all jobs were posted in the local paper and you had to sit back and hope the right people applied. Thank goodness. Today you can use online job sites, specialist recruiters, word of mouth and referrals and also tools like Linkedin. Do you know how to use 'Advanced Search' on LinkedIn? If you do, you can go to specific job titles local to you or the location you need the person in; you can search within the internal structure of competitors, you can define the length of experience and skill set you need. Combine all of the above tools to ensure your net is cast wide and deep.

Before you interview someone, do your research. Use those tools and social media more generally to find out about them. What public persona do they emit? How do they approach life? What are their real interests – not just the ones they add to their application? Who do you know or connect with that might be able to give you any information about the individual? This is not 'Big Brother', this is proper due diligence. For good candidates it is no issue, for those who want to mislead and/or exaggerate, the amount of public data out there today can be a real challenge. For my part I have been horrified a couple of times on checking out an individual who looked to be a 'strong' candidate.

Some tips for the interviews themselves -

- <u>Start friendly and informal.</u> You see people more accurately when they are relaxed.

- <u>Ask them what they know about you and your organisation.</u> If they haven't taken the time to find out about the company or about you, what does that tell you about their attitude?

- <u>Check for discrepancies</u> before you meet, between say, the printed CV, and their LinkedIn profile.

- I refer you back to chapter 10 on the subject of <u>'Questions'.</u> Use those techniques actively. If answers are general (*"Have you made your target every year at Acme?" Well, most..."*) then drill down to establish the real facts. If you are worried that it appears made up, or uncertain, leave it till far later in the interview and just repeat (*"sorry, I just realised I forgot to write it down earlier, was it 2 or 3 years you made your target at Acme?"*)

- Ask for examples. This applies to every job role interview, not just sales. Create scenarios for them to respond to. In sales for example you could ask some of these – *"Tell me about the deal you are most proud of?"* Or biggest, or most complex, game-changing etc. *"Imagine you join us and you are asked to open a new market for us. If there was no marketing support, can you tell me how you would approach that sector and what your steps would be to engage with it...?"* Then ask follow up questions to test their answers.

- Ask them some skill questions. Again, using selling for these examples. *"What do you understand by qualification and how would you apply it?"*. Of course, this can be used on any required skill for any role. *"What would your approach and strategy be in trying to open a new, major customer account?"* *"Explain your use of other team members to help deliver results."* There are thousands of questions like these. Perhaps aim them towards where you see a potential lack of experience. The manner and confidence of the answers to questions like these is almost (but not quite) as important as the answers themselves. In other words, do they cope well under pressure?

- If it is a frontline sales role and they have done well so far, and are coming back for a final session, I will often ask them to create and deliver a presentation – again, to look at the content and their ability to cope with a stressful activity. Subjects – *"sell us your current company/offerings"; "try to sell our company back to us"; "here is a scenario or subject, present to us on it..."*.

Finally, if you have carried out the interview and all seems well. If you have had another team leader or senior team member meet them too and have decided to make them an offer. ALWAYS, ALWAYS actually act on the references they have offered you. Contact them. For me, a refusal to give references, or even reticence, is a showstopper. But also try to find your own connections that might know them as well. Again, social media has changed this world too. Pre-set references are usually positive...

The Lesson
Once you are used to the process AND if you follow the steps and hints above, an interview can be an interesting and stimulating exercise. Never, ever, forget its importance to your success...

*"I hire people brighter than me
and then I get out of their way."*

Lee Iacocca

Notes

_____

_____

_____

_____

_____

_____

_____

_____

_____

_____

_____

_____

_____

_____

_____

_____

_____

_____

_____

_____

_____

15

Performance Measurement

*"If you can't measure it,
you can't improve it."*

Peter Drucker

In this chapter I will not use theory. This all comes from hard, sometimes bitter, experience over many years. Everyone prefers not to be measured. It makes life so much easier, doesn't it? All sales people (unless they are well ahead of their target, in which case this is 100% reversed!) are among the least comfortable with constant measurement. If they are ahead of goal then they want everyone to know! And more generally, people tend to not like specific targets and measures.

Setting sales targets can be a daunting thing to do at the beginning. Similarly, in any other role, there is a process to setting targets. It's really not too difficult...

First, note down what you want and need from them, for your team or business. In a small business or a corporate sales role, it is absolutely normal to set a numerical target. What revenues generated justifies their initial or continued employment? That's a good starting point but is it enough? A clearly defined performance plan, tied to their compensation plan (aka complan), with everything covered up front, is by far the best way to go. But what other elements, apart from the headline number should be considered and added in, if appropriate? Here are some to consider –

1. Is the overall goal to be based on bookings made (and what is the definition of that to you)? Purchase Order received, your Order paperwork signed, what if the deal includes non-standard contract terms and conditions? Or perhaps it might be bookings made and subsequent delivery completed (again, however defined), or is it a cash received target? Is it the headline revenue number you want measured, or just the gross profit, or the net profit? You need to consider what you want and the company needs, before laying out the complan.

2. <u>When do you pay commission out against orders</u> –
   and on what basis? If they have signed a contract
   for monthly payments do they get all of the annual
   revenue-based commissions up front or as it
   proceeds through the year? Or at some mid-point?
   Only for year 1 if it is a multi-year contract?

3. <u>What is the target based on?</u> Your core product,
   and/or supporting services? Professional services
   attached to the deal? Service contracts? Define
   clearly what counts towards the target number you
   have set. What rates are paid out against each of
   these elements?

4. <u>When?</u> If all the deals come in on the last month of
   the year is that OK for you? If not, define monthly or
   quarterly expectations (I have seen these also include
   ups and downs for the season – lower in mid-summer
   when the holiday season is in full swing for example).

5. <u>Priorities.</u> Perhaps you want a focus on a specific
   market, or on one of your offerings above the
   others. Maybe you need at least four new 'strategic'
   customers (again, define them) from this person,
   this year. Lay that out and emphasise it though your
   payment scheme too.

6. <u>Velocity.</u> It can often be helpful to measure velocity.
   What does this mean? Think of your pipeline as laid
   out in your CRM or even on paper. You have perhaps
   five stages and maybe (hopefully!) between at least
   two and twenty deals in each stage. Velocity, in
   this context, is simply the sum of the movements
   further along/down the pipeline in a given period,
   say a month. It is easy to create a measure and it
   does show clearly, just how well and quickly there is
   progress.

7. Finally, on all that I have listed, <u>what is the most important,</u> what is second etc? Make sure your plan leads them to your business focus areas first and foremost. Drive their behaviour.

8. I also include a couple of <u>'soft' measures</u> in the complan too. Just to focus minds. Things like work rate, working hours, being a professional team member, mentoring more junior staff etc.

9. I often ask the sales person to use the available ratios (see below) to <u>figure out their own activity level requirements.</u> In non-sales roles there will usually be process steps where the same thing can be done.

I think, from this small list, you can see that there are many factors to be considered in a tight and clearly defined complan. Spend the time on this – please! In the early stages of my career, I found that complans were often hurriedly assembled. Guess what, like water, salespeople will always find the easiest route to their earnings. And it's usually to your disadvantage if you haven't done your job right. I have seen a company confuse revenues with net profit – now that was a true disaster for everyone, except the sales team members. All of this means that, if you have the power to set or influence the complan, you must make sure the highest earnings come from achieving whatever is your highest business priority.

The complan is now set and the individual(s) has signed it. Do you leave it for a year? Of course not, that is where ongoing performance measurement comes into play.

Measuring and analysing performance is critical. It helps you to spot issues early on. They could be internal (lack of effort, product shortcomings etc) or perhaps the market you sell into has changed under your feet. Your speed of response as the leader is all important here.

For new employees, take the time to clearly lay out your expectations – not just against the numeric target(s) but also in terms of work rate, behaviour, ethics etc. Make it all clear from the beginning.

At the outset, get yourself a large whiteboard or similar. Put it up on the wall or in a prominent place. Then create a board recording the most critical goals your team has. Most normally in sales, the deals you want to close and each person's progress towards their monthly, quarterly or yearly target. List by salesperson and keep it simple. A strong, visual reminder of success, progress and what still has to be done.

Set aside times for one-to-one reviews of progress against the targets set. Don't let it falter. Everyone should know they will be reviewed and asked about their performance regularly. Remember those questioning and coaching skills I have already highlighted. In essence, what you are doing is creating what is known as a 'replicatable process'. Something that works, is understood and accepted as required, fair and reasonable. It is always more difficult to introduce after time has passed – the structure doesn't exist so this is seen as a burden. Upfront it's just part of the job.

One technique I have used consistently since the 1970's – to great effect – has been the measurement of ratios (aka Conversion Ratios). I have been a convert and talked about the concept for over 30 years now. It is a powerful tool for the salespeople themselves, but they are also invaluable to a 'switched on' leader. (And they can be applied in whatever discipline you are managing, as long as there are measurable steps in whatever process you are leading a team through). The idea is quite simple. CRM's record the deals and their details as they (hopefully) move through each step along your pipeline. And that is all well and good. But you can do so much more than just record basic facts...

It's not the basic data itself - *"how many deals are there in stage 2 or stage 3, what is their £/$ value?"*. Far more important to me than just those raw numbers is the idea of the resulting 'conversion ratio' between each of your sales stages. This was the big lesson I learned all those years ago – back in those days it was recorded on a daily sheet of paper rather than in a CRM. But the recording mechanism being used doesn't concern me, it's the hidden information in there that points to where the gold is sitting. Now take a break or walk around for two minutes because the next paragraph goes into real detail – but it is critically important!

Start with your end result in mind (typically the annual target number). Now look at your activity records. Then look at what they mean for you. Here's a simplified example. How many cold calls/social contacts/ engagements does it take you to achieve one real conversation with a qualified new prospect? That's Ratio 1. How many of these identified prospects does it take you to get to the next stage – let's say a meeting to review their needs in detail or a demonstration of your solution? That's Ratio 2. How many demonstrations then lead to an agreement to quote (or explore needs or whatever is your next stage). That's Ratio 3. Perhaps finally you ask, how many of these quotation stage deals do you need to close one sale. That's Ratio 4. Now using simple arithmetic and your average deal size, you can very easily figure out (if your historic activity records in the CRM are reasonably accurate) how many new, perhaps cold calls/ contacts a week or month YOU need to make to hit your annual target, how many demonstrations a month are needed, etc. How? Well let's assume there are just four steps and at each only 50% of deals move forward to the next step (a constant 2:1 ratio), and your average deal size is £75K then to get to a £500K target you will need 112 qualified deals at your first stage. Eh? Follow the process with me... You need seven deals at £75K to get over target (7 x 75K = £525K). But that is the outcome from stage 4.

With a 2:1 ratio you will need 14 deals at the final stage to close those 7, 28 at the stage before to get your 14, 56 at stage 2 and finally, 112 qualified prospects entering at the top of your funnel. Of course, this is just a snapshot picture and it's based on a very unrealistic set of ratios. After all, how many people have a hit rate as good as 2:1 on their first contact with prospects? Your own ratios may perhaps be something like 12:1 at the top, dropping hopefully to 2:1 or even 1.5:1 as you reach the very end and try to close the deal. The point is this. Knowing what those ratios are historically, tells you what has to be achieved at each step to get to your target. This is a powerful but infrequently used mechanism to define exactly how to achieve success. The elements are – time available, qualified deals entering the pipeline, those ratios at each stage and the average deal value. With that historic information, or even just starting today to measure in this way, you are in a better place to start reviewing and tuning your sales process.

So, what does this self-help concept have to do with team management? While it can make a fantastic difference to the individual that uses it, it is also a wonderful tool for guidance and early warning at the management level. Let's say your process is actually a bit more complex than the sample above. Perhaps six clearly defined steps. If you enforce measurement of those ratios you can clearly see where there is a poor dropout rate at any given stage. These ratios are typically viewed like this – 3:1, 2:1, 10:1 etc. Of course, you want them to be as close to 1:1 as possible. Lower means the deals are flowing along the pipe and not dropping out. Maybe you have a high number of prospects at the first stage but you lose a very large number of them before they proceed to your next formal 'Needs Investigation' step. Ask yourself 'why'? Is it a lack of skills in the team, something wrong in the sales approach, the way your current process is running, competitive activity etc? Dig down, focus on any steps where the ratio is poor and work to improve them. Slight improvements in the ratios will have an enormous impact on team success.

But even more important, you can then, as time passes, compare these ratios BETWEEN team members. How is it that Mary's conversion ratio at the first two steps is twice as good as anyone else? What is she doing differently? Have her talk at the next sales meeting – detailing everything she does to perform so well. And what about Simon, why is his ratio in closing the deals that do make it to the end of the pipeline so poor? Ratios enable you to quickly review real-world, day-to-day performance and make valid, logic-based, clear cut comparisons.

The Lesson
Repetition is the Mother of Skill. This review, analysis and coaching discipline needs to be ingrained into your management and leadership DNA from the outset. Check often and make corrections and give advice and support each time. And yes, pull them up when you see things that are wrong. It's easier to do that as you go along (like small corrections in a rowing boat) rather than ending up way off track at the end with no time to fix the problem. Putting off giving critical advice will only make it harder to adjust later.

"As a middle (or front-line) manager, you are in effect a chief executive of an organisation yourself, you can improve your group's performance and productivity, whether or not the rest of the company follows suit"

Andy Grove

Notes

Chapter

16

Time Management

"People are frugal in guarding their personal property; but as soon as it comes to squandering time, they are most wasteful of the one thing in which it is right to be stingy."

Seneca

Are you an organised person? Really? So, what does your desk look like right now? ☺

It's a self-evident, obvious, clear as day truth that if you use your time more effectively you will achieve more. I think most of us believe we use our time effectively. But do we, really?

I covered this subject from the perspective of the individual sales person in The B2B Selling Guidebook. Here's part of what I said then...

> "...our world is now more packed with distractions than every generation before us has coped with, added together. Recent research points to this generation as having the shortest attention span of any since measurement began – and we can all see the reasons why. TV (with how many channels?), entertainment on demand (catch-up, YouTube, Netflix et al), social media in all its guises, gaming, messaging apps, enticing websites for online entertainment, gambling and shopping, multi-media services, the power of the web itself. We are drowning in distraction, and trust me, I include myself here. My 30-year old self would not believe how I spend my time these days.
>
> Here's an example...
>
> Some people just REALLY get this. Long before all these above distractions added to the issue, one of my early bosses ran a very tight, hard ship. The sales team worked from an office in the basement of our branch operation. We had to record all of our different activities each day on a sheet of paper and total them up. About one day in three, we would hear the shout – just as the clock touched 5pm. *"Come on up and bring your sheets"*. These sheets recorded everything – cold phone calls made, successful calls, follow up calls, meetings, demonstrations etc. We would stand in a line in front

of his desk. After some general chat he would pick one person each time and the routine went like this...

"Irving, let me see your sheet". Of course, if chosen, your insides fell. He then read the sheet – and I very quickly found out that he had a fantastic calculating and analytic brain. *"So, Irving, you made 48 calls today – quite good. Of those you had six meaningful conversations. Well done – a good conversion ratio. Oh, and you did one demonstration in the demo room upstairs. That all sounds good, but hold on... 48 cold calls at say just over a minute each gives me around an hour. Six conversations at around ten minutes each gives me another hour. And a demonstration takes around an hour too. But let's be kind and say yours took a total of 1.5 hours. That adds up to 3.5 hours. So, now tell me what EXACTLY did you do for the rest of the day?"* At this point the poor chosen 'victim of the day' knew that whatever they said they couldn't fully account for their time. You felt that you had worked hard, you know you were busy, but somehow you could never explain that time. Of course, in reality things always took a little longer, you muddled around on unimportant tasks and the sales team chatted throughout the day. But the principle of focus and time management was hammered into us around once or twice a week without fail.

The conversation always ended the same way. *"So, Irving, you don't know what you did today. You wasted your time. Are you lazy or just stupid?"* And he forced you to answer in front of everyone! At the time, as a new, naive, but enthusiastic salesman, this was my worst nightmare – I am sure I woke up in the middle of the night having panic attacks about it. Looking back, I can smile and realise that a fundamental rule of good business was being forced into my brain – where it has stayed ever since. Reading this and thinking of today's business environment I guess some might say this was high pressure, perhaps almost bullying. I would strongly say the opposite. If you can't respond to and cope with pressure internally and in front of your friends and colleagues – on a subject you are actually living – how will you ever cope with difficult and demanding customers? This was good, practical teaching of a real, core business attribute and has served me well through the years."

Now, I think you might smile or laugh about that in terms of a sales person or another employee. But, what about you? Are you so much better? Are you effective, ineffective or maybe even a 'busy fool'? What is your time <u>invested</u> in (or are you just <u>spending</u> it without a care?)

Take some quiet time out and have a detailed look at your own time allocation. What percent of your time in an average day is actually productive? I would suggest that if you can reach 50%+ you are doing much better than average. We each need to review how we can optimise our productive time and remove those little, but multiple, distractions. Set rules for yourself. *"Online stuff only at lunchtime". "No more than 30 minutes on all social media between 0830 and 1800". "No meetings during core productive times."* Or whatever will make the difference for you. Then exert real effort to stick to that new regime. While your competition (internally and externally) is more and more distracted, become more focussed and effective.

As a leader you have two responsibilities. First, you have to become time efficient yourself, second you then need to coach and mentor your team to increase their effectiveness too.

I hope the section above will give you a starting point to work from. There are many theories on time management. It is, of course, very much tied up with your priorities and focus. I am always amazed by individuals who actually understand this, but then choose to waste their time on less critical work day after day. So, what can we do to improve our time management?

Some suggest segmenting your time – and sticking to it. Allocate a specific time to each type of task. Or, NOT doing certain things until all your catch-up work is done. No calls or meetings until 11am. That can be quite a useful discipline – if it works for you. Ideas and tactics only work if they fit you as a person.

You can also apply structure to your working week, as well as your days. Be available for joint visits, or customer meetings on set days. That leaves the other time free for you to prioritise your other work.

Allocate team or individual meetings – as much as possible – to non core times. First or last thing, over a working lunch, beginning or end of week...

Another tool is to set your priorities and then plan your time based on doing everything on the top priorities before anything else. Only after the critical and important is handled, does the rest get done.

As useful is another exercise a boss of mine taught me (above). For a few days make a note of the work you are doing (just on a sheet of paper beside you). After some time – recorded like this - has elapsed, look at each day and work out how much productive time you managed each day. How much time was devoted to your top 3 priorities? THEN ask yourself – honestly – what happened to the rest of the time. What filled it? Was it invested or just spent?

I have even gone a stage further with my teams. Four times since those days of old I have been working with a non performing team member. Each time, they seemed individually competent but were not getting results. I drew up a very simple one pager rather like the one I was subjected to all those years ago and asked them to fill it in daily, for a week. Each time I only put in as categories, what would be productive work in their roles. In selling for example I restricted it to cold calling including basic research, successful calls, proactive emails (at that time, no LinkedIn etc), demonstrations and proposals. I then had them total up the time on these tasks for themselves. Each time the total came to something like 30-40% of their working day. They then started to wonder themselves, what they were doing the rest of the time! And yes, every time, performance improved.

Here's a tip that has worked for me. When you are over busy do you ever find yourself thinking about work at night, not sleeping well, unable to focus? If so, get a private notebook and at the end of each working day note down everything you need to address tomorrow. And I mean everything. Check you have it all written down. THEN close the folder, put a rubber band around it and/or put it in a drawer or safe place until the next day. Then tell yourself that's it. You don't need to remember or let your brain keep on working on these actions, it's all there – and switch off. This has worked well for me over the years. Your brain needs time to wind down and relax, so make sure you work to create that calm.

The Lesson
Time Management is not an option. Far too often I have seen people who are chasing their tail, all day, every day, into the night. You can't work well if you are doing that. Dump everything you can – delegate or ignore. Prioritise what you have to do and then allocate your time in proportion to the importance of that action.

"Make use of time, let not advantage slip."

William Shakespeare

Notes

_____

_____

_____

_____

_____

_____

_____

_____

_____

_____

_____

_____

_____

_____

_____

_____

_____

_____

_____

_____

Chapter

17 | Priorities

"One cannot manage too many affairs: like pumpkins in the water, one pops up while you try to hold down the other."

Chinese Proverb

Priorities are self-evidently critical to your success. Do we actually know what our own true priorities are? Do we build our day, week, month and year around them?

Before getting into the details, have a look at the picture below, which I found recently. It was obviously created for fun but there is a real message in there. How often today is that new 'basic need' one of the first things we think of as we plan travel or holidays? Think about that for just a moment. Anyway, it both amused me and brought to the fore how we live our lives today. Why do I show the image? Well, consider how you address your own priorities. You can do this thinking against a fantastic and simple model created quite a few years ago now - Maslow's 'Hierarchy of Needs'. This well-regarded research points to a hierarchy in what we need to have in life. From the basic needs for life to the highest levels of expectation. Add 'Business' to the search and you will find multiple images of its application. The point? If you haven't covered the basics then the 'nice to haves' are of no interest. It powerfully applies to leadership and selling too!"

In effect, Maslow's Hierarchy states the very obvious. As humans, we first need the basics to sustain life – water, then food, then shelter and warmth. Only once all of these are achieved do we then move on to the next level in the hierarchy – safety. And so, we move onwards and upwards, hopefully...

Back to business! First and foremost, you can NOT have a large number of priorities. In the last decade, working closely with start-ups, I have found the need, several times, to sit down with the business leader and say to them "please tell me all your priorities". All too often, they are on point six – and accelerating fast – when I have stopped them dead. Priorities are just that, the MOST important things, and you can't have six, ten or twenty of them. So, the first step is to decide what your core, most critical priorities are.

Now, it's not to my mind an actual 'set in concrete' fact but I really, really like the idea of 'The Rule of 3". This is an old – but also at the same time, very current - idea on exactly how to set your priorities. It also works in many other areas of life. The idea and theory are simple, you can't have more than three areas of focus at one time. Three also seems to just be a maximum – and optimum – number. In storytelling, science and history, we see the '3 Musketeers', '3 wise men', '3 little pigs', 'Newton's 3 laws of motion', '3 acts in a play'. In public speaking, almost all of the greatest speeches of all time use the rule of 3 for their underpinning rhythm and cadence. In public health the vast majority of notices and guidelines give 3 symptoms, 3 rules, 3 steps. The concept can be traced all the way back to ancient Greece and has been consistently effective and applied in entertainment, writing, presenting and leading since then.

I am not religiously set on 3 as THE number, but boy it's the best place to start from. Take a piece of paper and set down your own three business, and then once again, your three personal priorities. Force yourself to stop at 3 in each category. Look again at them. Have you got it right? If you have, how much time and focus do you give to them? If you are struggling, step back and ask yourself how you define and describe your priorities.

The most memorable story on this subject was delivered to me as I studied for my MBA. One lecturer was teaching on the subject of priorities and he gave an analogy to explain really understanding priorities... *"Imagine you are on a commercial flight, crossing the Pacific. Exactly half way across with no land within 2,000 miles of you, the Captain tells you the engines are failing, and you will have to ditch! As you glide down towards the ocean there can only be one thought in your head... "Please let us 'land' safely". Somehow, miraculously, the sea is fairly calm, and the plane does indeed land and float for a few minutes. You get your lifejacket on and join the queue to jump into the sea. Again, there can only be one thought in your head... "Please let the lifejacket inflate". You jump and it does! The plane sinks, and you are now floating, legs down in the Pacific, with no rescue in sight. Now again there is only one possible thought "Please, no sharks!".* And that is how priorities work. When you were gliding downwards in the plane, the lifejacket didn't actually matter. When you were just leaving the plane, sharks didn't matter..." What a simple, but incredibly powerful lesson.

Sit down with your team and explain your priorities for them, why you have set them and how they are defined and measured. Ask questions to make sure they understand! Then observe and tune their behaviours. Watch your team as they work towards your stated priorities.

Take every opportunity to delegate. Give team members the chance to prove themselves, stretch their skills and experience, while of course freeing you to focus even more strongly on your priorities.

The Lesson

It is a really simple idea. Take the time to really clearly establish your priorities. Both for you and for your team. Then take time to yourself, every month, to measure your progress against them. Then discuss and share progress (or the lack thereof) with your team regularly.

"Things which matter most must never be at the mercy of things which matter least."

Johann Wolfgang Von Goethe

Notes

Chapter

18

Meetings, Meetings, Meetings...

"If you had to identify, in one word, the reason why the human race has not achieved, and never will achieve, its full potential, that word would be meetings."

Dave Barry

Ah meetings, don't we all just love them? They are so fruitful, fun and rewarding, aren't they? Not...

But meetings are an essential part of working life. Both internal and external, they give us structure and enable communication, problem solving and progress. As I write this chapter there is a lot of comment and debate about the new phenomenon of 'Zoom Meeting Fatigue'. It's just another stress factor in our world of meetings.

Take a moment and ask yourself what it is that annoys you most about meetings. Lack of clarity? Running over time? Wasting your time? No objectives? No clear outcomes? Behaviours? Those who don't contribute? Inattention? My guess is you could easily add a few to this list. Let's try to reverse them now. Here are some of my rules for effective meetings –

- Clearly agreed and communicated set up. Start time, end time, location, attendees.

- Always teach and enforce respect for time, your own and for each other.

- There <u>must</u> be an agenda, and it has to be issued early enough for attendees to read and absorb it.

- After a period, ad hoc items must come off the agenda. If they haven't been actioned, why not? If they just sit there what is achieved? Better to remove the item entirely.

- Purpose. Exactly what outcomes should there be.

- Who is leading the meeting? Who will take notes and record agreed actions?

- What decisions or actions need to be agreed.

- Of all the items, which are the 3 priorities?

- A clear understanding of what is expected and acceptable behaviour.

- Always issue a summary of the agreed actions – and owners – shortly after the session ends.

A few years ago, I came across this chart – designed to be displayed in rooms where meetings take place. I just can't remember where I first saw it but it is excellent. In two companies I put this up myself in the meeting room and also emailed it to all who would attend my meetings.

Could those guidelines be useful to you?

Now, as far as sales meetings specifically go, here are some of my thoughts – based on 43 years of good, bad and catastrophic!

- Allow for extra time. Pad the timings a little. Salespeople like to speak! Start with your own #1 priority. Probably a review of the numbers for the last period and forecast for the next. Then use the agenda to step down the priority scale.

- When someone gives a throwaway *"I missed my target last time, but I will be OK next month"*, don't accept it. Why? What happened? What can we change to avoid a recurrence? Not judgemental in tone, but leading towards continuous learning and improvement.

- Aggressively manage time. After a while people will know you are serious about arriving on time, keeping to time, finishing on time.

- Allow for fun. As I mentioned earlier, I used to start meetings with a very short quiz or activity.

- Give others responsibility. *"Jill, I want you to research and come to the next meeting with 3 ideas (of course!) for improving our qualification skills."*

- Follow up. This is so often forgotten. The meeting itself then becomes the end result. A meeting should always be an enabler – leading towards positive actions and progress.

- Take a little time, each time, to give advice, input and suggestions to the team. Allow for discussion around your comments.

I once ran a sales meeting with the 'big boss' in attendance. It went SO badly. I was mortified. Right from the outset everything overran and the timing just got worse and worse. In the end, and mid-sentence, he simply stood up in front of my team and announced *"We are now over the allocated time, the meeting is over, Jim come to my office please."* We weren't even half way through. Can you imagine how I felt? How embarrassed I was? And how scared I was about what was to come? He treated the problem perfectly in my opinion. It had been a disaster. But this is what leadership 'class' looks and feels like... As I followed him into the room he said *"Jim, I know we overran so much you haven't eaten. Go and get some sandwiches for us and come back in, and don't worry.*" I did as he requested, and was now more intrigued than worried. *"As we settled back in, he said "Well, that didn't go well, did it? Why don't we take half an hour and work through what didn't work together and figure out what we can do to change it in the future".* Quiet, calm, serious but not judgemental. PERFECT. Of course, he already knew exactly what I was doing wrong. He coached and mentored me and then didn't come into the next meeting (again, a great tactic, giving me time to try things and learn from the experience without the pressure of him watching) but he did attend the one after that. He just sat at the back and smiled... And that poster and all of the comments I make above? They are what I know now, from that session and the guidance I was given. That is what real - and classy - leadership looks like...

The Lesson
Meetings are a requirement, but they don't have to be a burden. Run properly and with the right planning and focus, meetings can be at the core of your success. Planned and managed badly, they can destroy morale and sap the will of everyone who attends them.

"The longer the meeting, the less is accomplished."

Tim Cook

Notes

_____

_____

_____

_____

_____

_____

_____

_____

_____

_____

_____

_____

_____

_____

_____

_____

_____

_____

_____

_____

_____

_____

Chapter
19

Discipline - and The Problem Child

"Discipline is rarely enjoyable, but almost always profitable."

Darrin Patrick

Discipline has always been one of the harder aspects of leadership. Most normal people just don't like confronting issues – and the knowledge of what will then likely result. Of course, there are those managers and leaders who just LOVE the shouting matches; screaming at their team, overriding everyone and always knowing best. I doubt any such creatures are reading this book - after all, they already know everything!

The root of the word 'discipline' is interesting in its own right. It derives from the Latin word 'discipulus' which means pupil or student. It is also, as you might guess, the root of the Christian word, disciple or follower. The dictionaries argue a fair bit, but there is a view that discipline is perhaps more about learning and setting standards, not so much around basic rules or punishment

For the majority of the population, conflict, pointing out issues and confronting problems is not a comfortable activity. So how best to prepare and do it? There is again absolutely no science in this chapter, just my own input and what has worked well. Of course, there are also early career horror stories in my own life where I didn't get it right...

Let's start with the basics. If you are to manage individuals and lead the team you can't do everything on a hunch. Let's say you have spotted a problem you need to address, run first through this checklist –

- Is this a performance or behaviour problem? Be careful to distinguish between the two. I have seen excellent performers who are disruptive and dangerous for the rest of the team. Their behaviour outweighed their contribution.

- If it's definitely performance, is it only this individual that's struggling or are more team members exhibiting the same shortfalls?

- If there are others, what are the common points? Is there anyone who is not impacted in the same way? If so, what are they doing differently?
- If there are others, are they all really dumb and incompetent (bad news for your recruitment and leadership skills!), or is there an external factor at play? Say, changing market conditions, lack of training, product shortcomings? If yes, then you need to put a resolution plan together to address the issues and support them to improve.

- If it does turn out to be just them and especially if it is a behavioural problem, think seriously about the right course of action. Maybe their activity rates are not comparable to other team members, or attendance is poor, lateness, lack of energy – all resulting in poor business performance. You could jump straight to a 'Formal Warning' action. But, really? Why not coach them, lay out what you have observed, give support and challenge them to improve. Offer extra help. If they don't change at all, then you move to the next step.

- BUT as you start to work with an individual who is exhibiting poor behaviour take some time before you jump right in with both feet. Look back at chapter 10, ask them questions. Dig into what is the cause. If they were a good hire, what has changed? Often when doing this I have found big issues at home or with their health. If you find that to be the situation, do the right thing by that team member. They will never forget it.

I have used a technique over the years which has been effective. Where someone is really not pulling their weight, or behaving improperly, I have taken them into an office. Quietly and clearly, I have laid out what I have seen. I then say, slowly and deliberately *"This... Behaviour... Is... Simply... Unacceptable... to... our... business...".* And then let the silence stretch. When they know you as someone who is generally supportive to them and a team player who always has their backs, this statement, delivered this way, leaves them quite shaken and in no doubt about what you think. That for me has in the past seen the problems stop there and then.

Those were some thoughts about the normal challenges. But what about the disruptor, the 'bad egg', the one who brings everyone down and will not change. At the start of my career, over 40 years ago, I twice saw such individuals literally being thrown out of the office into the street. Of course, that is absolutely not the right way to handle this situation but I can still look back and partly understand that frustrated, emotional response from their manager. This same process can also apply as you perhaps realise someone is simply not up to their job and there are no other options that you can find to help them.

What do we then do with our problem child?

If you are past the friendly chat stage, with no sign of adherence to your business and performance needs, then you step into a different world...

1. Make detailed written notes of the behaviour or performance issues. Dates, times, exactly what was happening, witnesses. What did you do to address it? Keep it all documented.

2. Set a 'Performance Plan'. In other words, a clear definition of what you and the company need from them – be it attitude, behaviour and/or performance. Set timescales and measurable objectives. Tell them clearly that you are putting them onto this personal plan. Then review progress (or the lack of it) with them exactly on time. Always send a memo covering your discussion straight after.

3. The reviews throughout this process should be frequent and planned – typically weekly. *"What did you say you would do last week?" "How did you do?"*

4. In fact, it can be useful to discuss exactly where the issues or shortcomings are and have the individual document and then set their own work and behavioural targets to overcome them. In such extreme cases it can be worthwhile treating them as you would an errant child or teenager. The first step can be just making them see for themselves what is wrong.

5. If the first objectives are achieved, then review with them, say well done and move forward – a bad chapter is closed. But make it clear that the process can be re-continued at any time. 'A shot across the bow'.

6. If the right progress hasn't been made then you have to start to become more formal. In this case you first have to get either HR, or external advice if you are in a smaller organisation. In every country I have worked in, there are strict laws around workplace discipline processes. In every country there was a requirement for clarity and enough time to effect the required changes.

7. In the UK, the formal steps – long since burned into the depths of my soul are – a) 'First Verbal Warning' which then has to be followed up with a written statement to them. This one always confused me, verbal but to be followed in writing! b) If the right changes have not occurred in a reasonable, defined timescale, a 'First Written Warning', and c) lastly a 'Final Written Warning'. In those last two steps it is far better to have a 'witness' there in these meetings. First because emotions can run too high and second,

to confirm the steps were followed correctly. That can be someone from HR, another unconnected manager or similar.

8. A note – I have ended up in a legal dispute, which I won. But this made me acutely aware of the need to both do the right thing and to be seen to do the right thing. Maximum help must be provided. And a reasonable timescale for change and improvement must be allowed at each step. Always think that the meeting, the written letter that follows and everything you say may be regurgitated in court, because it really might.

9. This is not a time for tempers or threats. This is perhaps the ultimate test of remaining calm and professional.

Finally, when discipline is required, or a team member behaves improperly, tempers can get raised. I was told many years ago that *"he who shouts first loses"* and I believe this to be true. So, in the midst of conflict or when things warm up too fast it is you, as the leader who has to calm things down, not incite as some managers do. Jeremy Pollack, writing for Forbes, makes some suggestions which I wholeheartedly endorse and paraphrase/add to below –

- First, tell yourself beforehand that you will not lose your temper. You are responsible for yourself.

- Under react. Often, individuals like this say or do something just for effect, to get attention and control. Don't give it to them. Not responding as they expect reduces their leverage.

- Use some form of internal phrase or mantra if things do kick off. Make up your own. He suggests *"Stay calm, don't react. Stay calm, don't react"* as an example.

- Have something visible - maybe on your desk - which serves to remind you of your approach and style. His suggestion? *"Calm, Caring, Curious".* What would yours be?

- Breathe! At the worst point, take a few seconds just to breathe.

- Finally, if it is out of control, call time on the 'conversation'. *"Let's take a break and reconvene once we have each had an hour to think about it..."*

The Lesson

All of the above are for the normal events and situations. Only three times in 43 years have I had to literally fire someone and walk them out of the building, confident that it was the only thing that I and the company could do. It was the dreadful reality of 'gross misconduct' and a particularly hard thing to do. BUT my point is this; whether it is a lengthy process or an out of the blue incident, think what will happen if you just ignore the problem and hope it will go away. This is the exact time that your team looks to you for example and leadership – don't let them down.

"A culture of discipline is not a principle of business; it is a principle of greatness."

James C Collins

Notes

_____

_____

_____

_____

_____

_____

_____

_____

_____

_____

_____

_____

_____

_____

_____

_____

_____

_____

_____

_____

Chapter

20

That Big Deal!

"What turns ordinary people into overachievers is the way they use their minds when they are called upon to perform."

John Eliot

From time to time, the 'deal of the year', the 'one we must win at all costs' comes into view. This principle also happens, in different ways, for any team - there is now and again, that giant, special challenge to be faced. The real leader needs to stand out and up front to literally lead when this happens...

Let me stick to the example of sales in its purest form. I have now lost count of these one-off deal situations but one or two will live with me forever. There are typically some common challenges. First, it's humungous. Second, it's complex. Third, it's a stretch but winnable. Fourth, we probably don't have enough time and/or resources and/or capability to do it justice. Do we walk away? You can, and sometimes that is exactly the right thing to do, but other times you just get that feeling... *"This could be the one".*

Running a sudden, timebound, incredibly challenging 'project' like this calls on your real leadership – and management – skills. You have to be engaged, setting the directions sometimes micro-managing, communicating very clearly and being positive but honest too. That is the theory, but what about the reality?

You have decided to go for it. Now you have a test for your leadership. This is a big one. Let's say you are running a sales branch or small business. You have to consider how to manage this priority. Take a deep breath and then jump in and lead! Let's assume it is big and complex and too tight for time; here is what I would do...

1. Who do we need in the team to fulfil and have the best chance of succeeding (say, for the proposal, solution development, emergency project or Tender reply)?

2. What are they doing at the moment? Who can cover for them?

3. What else can we delay or ignore to help give us the space to deal with this one?

4. Is there any other company resource we can call on to cover for us/help us? Now you have the team assembled and ready to go...

5. Create a working space, room, meeting room or whatever. Get a flip chart or whiteboard set up. Set overall project goals and daily/weekly ones. Get them up at the top of the board.

6. Assign tasks and be 'the enabler' as people work to achieve against them.

7. Delegate wherever you can to clear your time for leading and to develop your team members

8. Measure progress frequently and ruthlessly.

9. Make sure, from the outset, that you actually have a full team assembled or on call – sales, pre-sales, administration, finance etc. Treat them as equals in this one-off project team.

10. Remember chapter 6, the upside-down organisation chart? This is where you need to believe in and live it. I have led quite large teams working late into the night – and on to the next morning - to get the job done before a hard deadline. It was me, not the most junior member, who was out on the streets at 1am trying to find pizzas to refresh everyone. The others were too important to the task. And the smiles when I arrived back carrying five or six of them!

11. Once it is all done and the proposal or whatever is delivered, make sure you thank every individual and then organise some unofficial time off for them if you can, if it has been way over normal hours required,

especially for those who are not direct sales team members. I have, when the company refused to help, taken this ad-hoc team all out for drinks and food myself a couple of days later when everyone had recovered. After all, if you don't, what will the reply be the next time you ask for such a big favour!

12. Finally, if the deal is won, hold a big celebration and acknowledge everyone. In a larger company I have also written up a description of all that happened then said nothing until they each opened up the corporate newsletter a month or two later and saw their names up in lights there. Fantastic motivation for everyone.

The Lesson
Big projects or bids have the power to destroy or build a team. They can also create legends and team history! IF it's the right thing to do, never be half hearted about it. Go big or go home...

"You alone are responsible for what you do, don't do, or how you respond to what's done to you."

Darren Hardy

Notes

Chapter
21 | Qualification

*"The biggest room in the world
is the room for improvement."*

Helmut Schmidt

Why on earth would I be talking about qualification in a sales management book? Because it is vital for the manager to know as well as their team does, exactly how, when and what to qualify. Leading by example is critical when it comes to qualification.

Qualification is, put simply, one of the most critical core skills in selling, and its importance is, all too often, misunderstood.

Let's start from the basic question, 'Why'? I addressed this in my first book at the individual salesperson level –

> "Now, many salespeople say to me *"Of course I qualify, I do it all the time. I don't need a process or form to help me".* They are plain wrong. Proper qualification needs you to consider all the factors at play. I have been on countless visits with good – and great – salespeople but have never met anyone who can remember to query every possible factor or area that could impact the deal. There are just too many. That's where a simple process, in support of your creativity, skills and experience, is invaluable.

> This chapter is not a sales pitch for one of the available qualification tools against another. I really want to raise awareness and to have you actively seek out yourself the one that fits you best. And boy, is there a choice available!

> Stepping back a lot of years for a moment – It was away back in the mists of the end of the 1970's/early 1980's and I was sent on a training course by my employer. The trainer was running a detailed course on selling. The section that caught my interest however was the 1-page qualification tool – 'SCOTSMAN' – a mnemonic for the eight areas he believed you had to review and measure to increase your chances of success. It was simple, fast and elegant. And it helped me! Fast forward ten years

and I was starting work with another vendor. They had also adopted SCOTSMAN but theirs had been adapted in conjunction with the trainer to precisely fit their needs. I still have both these original sheets today. This tool has since been very widely adopted and adapted world-wide. It is used – and customised – across lots of industries. Looking on Google today I found over 130,000 articles and images with individual variations of the original single page concept. Widening the Google search to the more general 'Sales qualification tools' today yields 45.5 million hits. Titles like BANT (an even simpler tool, credited I believe to IBM in the first instance), TAS Qualification, ADOPTED, CUTE, MEDDIC and CHAMP pop up, along with many others. Each has its own strengths and uses. The point is this. Whichever of these mechanisms you review, analyse and then adopt, having a single way to measure likelihood (so what exactly does 80% likely to close mean to you, to your colleagues, to your manager? How do you define it?) and to look at the gaps in your knowledge so you can qualify better – or out – will always improve your deal closing percentage. It will also lead you to focus on the deals that are actually winnable and help you see past the natural optimism of the salesperson! I cannot emphasise the importance of professional and logical qualification enough.

Not only does the use of a qualification tool help you win more business, deal by deal, but you will also be able to more easily spot the areas where you tend to stall or lose. You can then consider your skills and approach and develop and focus your efforts to improve in those 'problem' areas."

So, qualification is a critical tool for the salesperson. Surely to lead, advise and support your team you must know at least as much, and preferably a whole lot more, than they do on this subject?

Do what I suggested in the above comments. Look at your

business, research the tools available and find the one that works best for you and your team. Then learn it inside out, back to front and use it every day. Make it the common language for the team. You should be able to shout across the room *"Anne, what is the Acme bid at today?" "Jim, it's now at 47!"*. You and she must understand exactly what that number or percentage means to both of you. A strong qualification tool will enable you to use shorthand against the status and likelihood of each deal.

You can also use qualification as a gateway to each step in your pipeline in your CRM. *"Nothing gets to the third step unless it is over 32",* or 50%, or 7 out of 10 or whatever scoring scheme you adopt. Selling is complex. There are almost innumerable combinations of situations to consider. <u>Make it simpler.</u> Applying some simple science and commonality means that all your team members can understand, measure and communicate much more easily.

When you then lose that big deal, as you always will at some point, you also have a ready-made framework for the win:loss review. It is important that everyone involved can learn and adapt after you experience a big – perhaps unexpected – loss. Ignoring it and going for the next deal, in the same way, is simply not a good plan. This 'Continuous Improvement' attitude will pay dividends. Not with shouting and accusations but reviewing the facts and looking for lessons learnt. Looking back also becomes easier when you can easily visualise and compare the steps taken – for better or worse.

The Lesson

Never leave qualification to the team, become a real guru yourself and practice what you preach. Lead by example and aim for real, continuous improvement.

"If you quit on the process you are quitting on the result."

Idowu Koyenikan

Notes

Chapter

22 | Customer Service

"Customer service shouldn't just be a department; it should be the whole company."

Tony Hsieh

Customer service is one of the core measures for any organisation. It applies equally internally and externally. For example, an admin team will have customers – those who use their services and receive their outputs. In a larger organisation, the legal department also exists to serve customers – in this case it is most likely those who interact with their customers and suppliers. But it is in sales and post-sales support that we tend to look at customer service most closely.

I have been very lucky, purely by chance, to have experienced the internal mindset of world-leading customer-oriented organisations. Is there value to delivering outstanding service? Of course, there is. Some try to prove their value through measuring 'customer satisfaction'. That's better than nothing. But far better, as Sequent believed, is to aim for customer success. After all, who ever saw a customer whose partnership with you ended in great success being unsatisfied? And conversely, when what you deliver is unsuccessful for them, how can there ever be customer satisfaction? 'Customer satisfaction' is just the measure achieved from customer success or the lack of it – so the aim must be to deliver success to your customers - first and foremost.

This concept is referencing a truly exceptional company (long since bought out by IBM) that I worked for. They were fanatical about true customer service. In addition to the principle described above, they lived by delivering far superior customer service. Now, I know you are thinking (or even saying aloud!) *"I know it is important, but WE deliver good customer service too".* Well, to my mind there is customer service and <u>flat out, genuine, world-class</u> Customer Service. Some examples of just what this means in the real world –

- A local customer suffered a large increase in their computer workload. Their systems pretty well stalled. The Branch team jumped in, immediately stripped their own office 'Demo and admin' Systems down and installed their memory and processing power free of charge at the customer site to improve performance – with no paperwork, request, commitment or process. These were not PC level systems; they were powerful enough to replace small mainframes. This was a substantial, high five figure lump of technology. When the customer asked about paperwork they just said *"get over your crisis and when it's all calmed down, I am sure we can sort something out..."* No authorisation or permission, the culture literally revolved around doing the right thing for the customer.

- Everyone in one organisation had to be able to define, on demand, who their customers were, no matter their role. AND what they were doing to improve their service to them.

- The manufacturing plant in one organisation, worked under perhaps the most extreme example of this approach. ANYONE, in manufacturing, R & D, or even a technical support person in a field office who found a major issue that could impact a customer, could literally 'switch a light on' and manufacturing stopped until it was fixed and the light went out. Yes, really. How often do organisations know something isn't truly perfect but it's still 'good enough' to go out. This was the exact opposite. The required team was instantly assembled to confirm, then resolve the issue, and they didn't leave the building until they had finished. They didn't queue for food in the canteen. They came together – as required – and worked till it was fixed.

Today, when I ask people about their differentiators, they often say 'our people are the best and we provide great customer service'. I must be truthful; I sometimes die just a little inside when that is said, having seen REAL world-class customer service centric businesses operating. And, of course, it was a privilege to sell and lead a small team selling those solutions against the big-name giants. How confident would you be with that team and ethos behind you? How sure, that you actually were the best? What do you think the customers thought of this supplier? Everyone selling in the market said *"we have good customer service"*, but once the prospect tasted this level of customer service it was often game over. Just imagine taking your prospect for a customer visit, knowing the experience they had with your organisation.

Finally, another great company sold some of the world's most powerful computers, each one running hundreds or thousands of simultaneous users. They were literally the core of the corporations that ran them. When a customer declared and reported a problem, they acted completely opposite to all normal Customer Services dogma. You know, 'the whole goal is to get that Service Ticket closed'. The support specialists are each normally measured – and rewarded - on how quickly each ticket is closed off. Not at this company. Once raised, the only person who could close a ticket off? The customer themselves. No pressure, no suggestions, no targets. Only when the customer decided it was definitely gone for good did the case get closed. Guess what their satisfaction ratings were like? Yes, off the scale.

Now, you might say *"but I am not working in high value, critical tech solutions."* You might think *"these things are for the big boys only"*. You are wrong. In the B2B Selling Guidebook I shared a story about the most powerful example of this idea I have ever heard. And I heard it directly from the person who lived it – a grocer of all people!

> I was once (at a sales kick off meeting) privileged to hear a speaker from the then self-proclaimed 'World's best supermarket'. The small, local supermarket group (today with six stores in New York State and Connecticut) was

called Stew Leonards. They coined their two rules of business which have become famous all over the world since they introduced it.

They believed in it so much they carved it on a 3-ton stone outside their first store –

Rule 1. The customer is always right
Rule 2. If the customer is ever wrong, reread rule 1

And they actually meant it...

Major, large name competitors put in their best store managers from elsewhere and offered special pricing and offers against them, but none could dent their position in the local market. A Director in our company (who had sponsored the talk) told how he and his young family had moved to a new house and arrived with nothing to eat. Late at night he and his family found Stew Leonards and bought a very large basket of food. At the till he realised he had left his wallet in his new home. *"No problem"* said the teller, *"Here's the receipt, pop back when you are sorted and pay us then"*. Could you imagine your local supermarket teller having that ability or authority? The speaker told us the story of a customer who broke a tooth on a baguette they had sold. They came in and asked if the carving on the stone outside was true. The supervisor said *"Yes"*. *"Well, here's the bill for $200 to fix the tooth"* - and they paid it! The loyalty they generated from their customers was incredible. Nothing anyone else did could persuade them to go elsewhere. Imagine being a big player's store manager being parachuted into this area to 'sort things out' – how could you compete? If you were 3% cheaper for a few weeks would the local population drop a retailer like that and move to you?

In that talk, our guest speaker then mentioned the concept of valuing the customer. He explained that *"If a customer with a bill for $25 is complaining, don't get upset about the $25 and what they want fixed compared to it, even if it costs far more. Imagine they have a post-it note stuck to their forehead with $104,000 on it. That's what the average customer will spend here ($100 a week) over 20 years, not to mention all their family, friends and colleagues added on top!"*

Did it work? Well, the company was incredibly profitable too. In 1992, Stew Leonard's earned an entry into The Guinness Book of World Records for having *"the greatest sales per unit area of any single food store in the United States."* Do look them up and read their story...

But why on earth am I ranting on about this? Just take a step back for a moment and consider all of the above stories. Who sets the approach to customer satisfaction and standards for your team? You do. Who leads by example and creates the atmosphere? You do. Who sets the rules and approach to Customer Service? You do. Even if you are but a small cog in a giant organisation, who interprets and exceeds the standards and rules set? You do. You own Customer Service for your internal and external customers. Oh yes, and two more things –

1. When there is a problem don't run away. There has been a lot of research done on this and the results are consistent. The happiest customers are NOT those for whom everything has worked smoothly and well. No, it's those who have suffered a big problem and whose supplier has delivered, fixed, excelled for them. Those are the biggest advocates you have. So, when your team face an unhappy customer problem, enjoy the challenge and the turnaround. It changes everything...

2. Go back to that upside-down organisation chart. Who are your own customers? Perhaps your actual customers of course, but surely also other internal departments and your own team members. What are you doing to improve what you do for them?

The Lesson
REAL Customer Service is a big part of the 'secret sauce' inside sustained success and competitive advantage – for the business and for you personally. Never ignore, minimise or belittle it. This attitude and service level does not belong 'in Customer Services'. Sales, marketing, admin, finance all have a big part to play. Every interaction with your organisation should have this quality shining through it. Delivering real customer service plays a big part in others deciding if they will even become your customers. Going above and beyond in the engagement process will deliver a sample of what you are like as a company.

"Good customer service costs less than bad customer service."

Sally Gronow

Notes

Chapter

23

Sales and Marketing. Best Friends or More Like Cat -v- Dog?

"The difference between sales and marketing is that marketing owns the message and sales owns the relationship"

John Jantsch

I approach this chapter as a Fellow in both the CIM (marketing) and in the ISM (sales management). I have worked 100% focussed in each of these disciplines separately, and at a high level. I have also run joint sales and marketing teams in multiple organisations. Sometimes you find an organisation where sales and marketing operate hand in hand, delivering incredible joint value. But frequently I have found discord and distrust. With my CIM hat on I have heard marketing professionals disparage and insult their sales colleagues. I also recently heard a very senior sales leader say that *"marketing is a pure cost centre, they have never done anything for me..."*. What's the reality?

First, I believe it is critical as you move along the path to achieving success, that the sales and marketing teams can and do work together, each bringing their own value to the table. The delineation has become less clear over recent years. Now we have Customer Service Reps (CSR's), Sales Development Reps and Business Development individuals/teams operating somewhere in the middle. But at their core, sales and marketing, however defined, are both complementary and essential. You cannot 'magic' up market awareness and visibility from a sales perspective. Leads are harder to gain if it is a solo sales activity to find them. Life is much more difficult without visibility, awareness, PR, events, product marketing, podcasts, social media marketing, campaigns, collateral and digital marketing in all its forms. Similarly, marketing will not succeed in generating revenues without the associated sales expertise and effort.

As a slight side-note... Marketing is much more visible as a profession and that, to me, is both a worry and wrong. In these times of enforced isolation, I decided to carry out some primary research into sales and marketing in the UK from a professional awareness and perception perspective. I have always felt that society, at least in the UK, seems to accept or admire marketing quite readily, but looks down on selling. So, I went online and looked for undergraduate (1st Degree) courses in the UK that focussed on marketing or sales in 2020. The results, quite simply, astonished me. Here is what I found through my searches...

According to the Guardian's University Guide 2020, there are more than 500 undergraduate courses in the UK with a major/core marketing component, that is, marketing led. While some are combined with related fields such as economics, psychology, design or fashion, there are also a lot of 'pure' marketing degree courses. There is a total of 2,809 courses across 133 institutions covering "management, marketing and business". On searching, I quickly realised there isn't even a search category or sub-category in the University Guide for sales!

Nothing came up for sales in any of the official guides I could find. So, I reverted to "pure google". I found one University advertising four sales degrees. However, on digging into the site, each one is actually entitled 'Sales and Marketing' – the content seems about even. Another University offers a 'Sales and Marketing Management' degree – same story. Three more universities advertise sales degrees, but on getting into the detail, one says its management course can lead to a career in selling, the others, again, offer marketing degrees with varying amounts of sales content. So, on reflection, I would suggest that to say there are 5 real sales degree courses in the UK is actually being pretty optimistic.

For the UK then, my research comes up with 500+ marketing degrees, 2,809 'Business, Marketing and Management' degree courses. And 5 'Sales' courses. Really? Seriously?

With that differential embedded into the education system it's no wonder that marketing is perceived in a totally different way to sales. I don't have an axe to grind but I am evangelical about improving standards in sales and sales management. Not so much in marketing. Why? Well, just look above – there is already plenty of support and activity geared to helping all marketing areas and disciplines improve. Lone voices like the ISM deserve much more support from government and education to raise the voice of sales than they receive today...

Sales and marketing are critical to any business. They are co-dependent, they should be synergistic. Just remember that marketing should own the messaging, sales the relationship. One starts the process, the other - hopefully – finishes it by opening up a new long-term relationship. How then should someone running a start-up, SME or sales team look at and manage this need for joined-up effort?

First, it is critical that sales and marketing objectives are aligned from the outset. They will not succeed in isolation. If you manage both, then it is all down to you. Carve out adequate time for both teams. Ensure they do join up and work together. If you don't own both, then co-operation with your marketing peer is entirely your responsibility. Don't ever wait for guidance or direction. You and your marketing equivalent should be joined together in all aspects of strategy and tactics. You need to understand and agree your joint goals and objectives and work to support one another. Is your sales team ready for the next marketing campaign? Does marketing know where your team have been gaining the most traction recently?

All of the above requires open, honest and trusted communication. You have to set the example and lead. Show respect for marketing, give them time in every sales meeting. Take their advice and input. Life gets a whole lot better when you work together towards that common goal.

The Lesson

Marketing can add enormous value to sales efforts and make life easier for the sales team. Never ignore or compete. Use their skills and capabilities to reinforce and support you in meeting your targets. Make life easier!

"I do believe the modern sales leader has to be a marketer."

Matt Gorniak

Notes

_____

_____

_____

_____

_____

_____

_____

_____

_____

_____

_____

_____

_____

_____

_____

_____

_____

_____

_____

_____

_____

_____

Section

3

Improving...

Chapter

24

Are you Really a Leader?

"The pessimist complains about the wind. The optimist expects it to change. The leader adjusts the sails."

John Maxwell

Just how appropriate is the above quote for these Covid-19 times? You have started (or reset) your relationship with your team. You have set standards and adopted techniques to measure progress and manage results. You are running effective meetings. You have the skills to improve performance and to manage disruptive individuals.

Now we start to address how to improve the direction of your team and enable them to over perform...

Remember the person I referred to in Chapter 11? The one who gave me the description of a leader? *"The one who decides which ladders are to go up against which buildings?".* This individual also taught me a great lesson, while I was thinking there was a problem with his behaviour!

I worked closely with him, he led the whole corporation for Europe, the Middle East and Africa (EMEA). I was responsible for roughly half of the sales revenues under him. We sat close to each other in the HQ building. About once or twice every two weeks I noticed him heading off at around 3pm. No meetings, no appointments, nothing. It really concerned me. He was a great leader, surely, he wasn't what we in the UK call a 'skiver'. Someone who doesn't work a full shift, or do what they should do? One day as we chatted privately in his office, I asked him outright what was happening. He smiled and then, in a totally relaxed way, explained an important truth that has guided me for the best part of 22+ years now.

"It's simple" he said. *"Everyone in this large organisation is working to achieve what I set out for them"* (the buildings and ladders analogy from earlier). *"My life in the office is packed with meetings, priorities, interruptions, crises and dramas. When exactly do I get the time to sit and think about what we all need to do? What should be done next? What has to change? Are we moving ahead of our market, or falling behind? How are we doing against the other worldwide regions inside the company? What could*

we learn from them? How is my SMT (Senior Management Team) doing? Well, now you know what I am doing when I head away early – it's to go home and sit quietly and think and plan." Genius! I then realised as I quietly watched on, that the next day after each 'early finish' he came into the office with a large sheet of actions, requests and directives.

A manager manages. But a leader leads, sets the direction of travel, brings in the big new ideas, makes the necessary changes and creates a positive direction and culture. This all takes time! Don't ever apologise for investing time in this side of your responsibilities. If you are acting, say in a start-up, as both a leader and manager, when EXACTLY do you take the time to think about the bigger picture? Or, are you always submerged? Think for a minute right now. What percentage of your working time do you devote to high level thinking and planning? WHERE do you go to do the thinking? Never in the office, it just will not work. HOW do you plan and think in this time? If you don't get your act together who is going to do it for you or help you? No one, because no one else can.

The Lesson
Take the time to lead. Make the time to plan...

"The very essence of leadership is that you have to have vision. You can't blow an uncertain trumpet."

Theodore M Hesburgh

Notes

_____

_____

_____

_____

_____

_____

_____

_____

_____

_____

_____

_____

_____

_____

_____

_____

_____

_____

_____

_____

_____

_____

Chapter

25

Find Your Own Path

"To know what one ought to do is certainly the hardest thing in life. 'Doing' is relatively easy."

Maria Mitchell

There is so much advice out there these days! Self-help books and podcasts, books, websites and podcasts on selling and on management and leadership, the list goes on. This book is part of that deluge too.

At some point though, you have to truly decide who you are and what you stand for. There is a real need to decide what, how and when you will lead. Not follow the advice of others – including me – but really, deep down for you.

I have talked a lot about those who influenced me for good. I owe each and every one of them a very large debt. Each great piece of advice, teaching by example and ethical leadership behaviour has helped me along the way. So has all of the bad practice, screaming matches, dreadful behaviour too. I think, in a way, I am also grateful for that as well. Being able to compare both is truly powerful for an individual. But, somewhere along the way I realised and just knew where I sat, what I wanted to be, how I wanted to act.

We all tend to just meander along in life, don't we? We react and adapt to what life presents to us. When exactly do we stand up and say *"This is me, this is what I stand for...?"*

I recently found a wonderful video on YouTube. A young guy from Scotland was laughing so hard he could hardly speak. Why? He lived in a typical suburban street. Like most of us in these enlightened days, his local town council had introduced a number of different recycling bin collections. Each was colour coded. You know, green for garden waste, blue for dry recycling etc. Anyway, he had been at a loose end and wondered what would happen if he put out the wrong coloured bin, and on the wrong day! His laughter became obvious when he pointed his phone camera out of his window only four hours later. There it was, a row of the wrong bins in front of every home, on the wrong day! They had each just blindly followed the visual message in front of his house and copied him without thinking for themselves. I did wonder what his neighbours thought when they realised later what he had done to them. But there is a real, serious message for us all there...

You often know when something isn't right, doesn't feel right or is not being done right. But usually the temptation is to just 'let it go'. Do you follow along and put your 'business bin' out too, because everyone else has, or do you think for yourself?

One of the most critical roles for a leader is to provide... leadership. How can you do that if all you do is follow? So, are you happy to take the easy path and just be a manager? Many, probably most, do exactly that. But the real joy and achievement comes to you only when you lead. And by the way, that can be in sales or other 'management', or at home, with your extended family or in church or social settings. Most of my regrets in life are because I didn't do something to fix an issue – I let it go.

So, this short chapter is a wake-up call. Take stock and, if you want to be a leader, decide who and what you are. Where are your red lines (and what will you do if someone crosses them)? On that point, I have taken the view that, in the panic of the moment, let's say with a difficult moral choice, it's way too late if you try to make a decision then. It's far better to think of what could happen, say at work or even on a night out, and decide exactly what your red line is, and your response would be, in advance. Then when the time comes, you already know how you will react, it won't be rushed and most likely the wrong decision.

The Lesson
What are your life and business goals and are they
written down? A leader can only lead if they have a goal
and direction. So, make them specific and review them
frequently. If for no one else, then at least for you.

*"Stop being who you were and
become who you are."*

Paulo Coelho

*"Regrets for the things we did can
be tempered by time; it is regret
for the things we didn't do that is
inconsolable."*

Sydney J Harris

Notes

_____

_____

_____

_____

_____

_____

_____

_____

_____

_____

_____

_____

_____

_____

_____

_____

_____

_____

_____

_____

_____

Chapter

26 | REAL Social Selling/ Marketing/ Business

"How you sell matters. What your process is matters. But how your customers feel when they engage with you matters more."

Tiffani Bova

The world is full of 'Social Media' and 'Social Selling'. Linkedin, Twitter, Facebook, Instagram all serve to connect people and interests. Some, like Linkedin, can be very useful in helping you navigate your business world. But there is another type of 'Social' that is often overlooked these days. Another form of 'Social Selling' or communication.

If you are leading a team selling or marketing commodity items at very low cost then this likely isn't for you. But, for those working in the complex and/or big-ticket world this works very well.

Several times in my career, leading teams selling into difficult markets I have gone a big step beyond the typical sales activities in support of the team and our objectives. I found great success from my attempts at this form of social selling.

Everyone tends to think of activities like golf or sports matches when planning 'customer entertainment'. The first time I did this, I researched instead what my customers – and their partners - liked. I found out quite easily that there was an interest in 'light' classical music. This wasn't a big interest of mine but I quickly found that an entry level sponsorship deal enabled me to have tickets for four to perhaps six concerts a year at relatively low cost. For up to date information of a typical example see the one I connected to – The Scottish Chamber Orchestra – (www.sco.org.uk). I set out my target list and issued a purely social, no business, invitation for target contacts and their partners to join my wife and I at a concert. Always just the four of us. A nice early dinner together, followed by a concert – and often a visit afterwards from the orchestra leader or conductor with NO business discussed. We just enjoyed a lovely evening. Almost every time my business target then said *"You must pop in and see me next week"* or similar. We had connected as people, not as business contacts. They were more open to me; preconceptions were removed and a warm relationship ensued. This is true social selling. At other times it was an unusual sporting event, not one of the usual 'standards', or something else of special, local interest.

The best single example? I had paid some money into the orchestra for a year or two and one day, out of the blue, they contacted me. *"Would you be interested in the train this year?"*. I was confused, it was an orchestra, not a travel company. It turned out that each year they rented an old, historic steam train and took it for a run into the depths of the Scottish Highlands and then ran an open-air, private concert. During the journey duos, trios and quartets wandered along the train delivering quick, fun impromptu music – classical, jazz and pop. Food and drink were provided too. I said *"yes please"* and started making contact with my friends and business contacts. What do you think the reaction was? In the end I had to hire two full carriages of the train. It was at a weekend so people met up the night before, socialised and we all then joined together for the big day. It was fun, memorable, and again 100% social. Everyone laughed, sang, joked and teased each other as the day progressed. What level do you think my business relationship with those big hitters was now? Yes, I had a lot of fun, but were my team more successful afterwards? Were we also seen as supporting the local community? All positive aspects of this social selling approach.

An interesting 'by the way'. The journey, from Inverness to Kyle of Lochalsh in Scotland is one of the World's great railway journeys. An incredible day out. Tripadvisor seems to 'quite like it', so look it up and imagine all of that with friends, great music and food...

What is there in your geography that is reasonably low cost, different, ethical (!) and fun? You may be surprised at what you can do to support your community AND improve your relationship with your customers and prospects.

The Lesson

This one's really easy. Just go and try it. Actually work to create (or use) a forum to get to know your customers and prospects better personally. And if you do, please let me know what you find wherever you are in the world! I firmly believe that in a post (or even controlled) Covid world individuals will relish these interactions even more.

"Sales is not about selling anymore, but about building trust and educating."

Siva Devaki

Notes

Chapter

27 | Improving Team Performance

"It always seems impossible until it is done."

Nelson Mandela

This chapter focusses on bringing together some of the actions we have already discussed. You are responsible for your team's performance. No one else. The quality and depth of your leadership and coaching will either sink or raise performance. Here are some thoughts on the subject that just don't seem to fit in anywhere else!

1. **Positivity.** If you walk in, weighed down by the load and not happy with life what message does that send? Now, I have seen cases of manic, crazy, over optimistic positivity in my career. That's absolutely not what I mean here. But you can set the tone, lift spirits and lead well. You have to learn from failure. Perhaps your team has just lost a big deal. Take a minute to be unhappy, then move straight on to a <u>positive</u> post mortem. What did we do badly? What did the competition do better? What can we change next time around? Doing this ensures you will keep learning and lose less deals as time goes on. As a leader, you should encourage and enforce this immediate review – from a positive perspective. Of course, losing a deal is hard, but you can at least deliver learning each time. And yes, if you have impressed but failed, it is absolutely OK to ask the prospect to give some feedback and advice. I had once or twice such individuals come into our office to talk it through with our losing team. We learnt a lot those days.

2. **Realism.** You need to be positive but, as I say above, not over the top. If things are difficult, your team need to know. Teams just hate not knowing the situation. As much as you are able, tell them the truth. I have had to address failing teams several times. It's not easy and a horrible thing to have to do. However, until they know where they are and what could happen if nothing changes, how can they start to respond and improve? With individuals it is always best to give such news face-to-face. Make it factual and clear. For

teams, let them all know at the same time, exactly where they stand – the best outcome and the worst. Then lay out your thoughts and ideas to improve. In the corporate world I have set out the basic reality of the money flow. (Look back at chapter 8). I have said *"here is the money we are generating and here is the cost of our operation. What do you think?"* In my experience people are not dumb. They look at that arithmetic and immediately understand the possible implications. The critical thing is to instantly get them working on plans and actions to turn things round.

3. **The worst news.** What do you do when all you have tried has not worked, perhaps the company is struggling and layoffs have to happen? I have been there too. First, again, never forget that people are people. They have their lives, their families, their goals and aspirations. That moment, when the worst career news is delivered – to anyone – is crushing. I have always tried to make sure I was there for each individual on the day. Where the process was just too big, I made sure whoever was representing me was properly briefed and knew up front exactly how I wanted it handled. But there is no way round it, it's just the worst thing you can ever have to do in business. So, do it with honesty and respect, putting the individual first.

4. **Competition.** I have always encouraged competition and a little rivalry amongst the team. League tables, spot prizes, plaudits all have their place. Just beware going overboard. I have seen individuals being berated for not being top at that precise moment. Team members called wasters in public. Competition should only ever be positive and encouraging.

5. **Praise.** As humans we all have our favourites. We just like some individuals more than others. One of the worst things a manager, never mind a true leader

can do, is to let that bias show through. It is difficult but you MUST be fair and equally supportive to all your team members. It's hard. I know from my own experiences. But it is also vital. Give public praise and congratulations every time you can. Make individuals feel special. Praise, given equally, is a powerful tool for a leader.

6. **Counsel.** Where you have a strong performer who starts to falter, don't jump up and down. Don't make a fuss. I have found that sitting privately, reviewing their achievements and just asking a leading question often gets to the cause or situation very quickly. *"Last year was incredible for you and the first half of this year was too. I am sensing a bit of a drop off at the moment and wonder what we can do together to get you back to where you should be?"* Followed by silence...

The Lesson

I don't want to labour this one, as I said in chapter 24, you need to figure out and then do, what is right for you. The above six items are just my thoughts, but they have all worked well for me in very different circumstances. The critical message is this. Don't let yourself, or your team, meander. You have the responsibility to lead and to spot what's happening. Figure out how you can improve performance and then devote time and effort to doing just that...

"The difference between a successful person and others is not a lack of strength, not a lack of knowledge, but rather a lack of will."

Vince Lombardi

Notes

_____

_____

_____

_____

_____

_____

_____

_____

_____

_____

_____

_____

_____

_____

_____

_____

_____

_____

_____

_____

_____

Chapter 28

Lead from the Front

"Leadership and learning are indispensable to each other."

John F Kennedy

In chapter 21, when I discussed 'That Big Deal' I mentioned how I worked with the team when it was literally 'all hands to the deck'. Heading out into the depths of the night and being the one to find and buy pizzas for the team did a little to ensure everyone felt valued and important while they were under extreme pressure.

But is there more you can do? Of course there is...

I have already talked about my strong belief in the idea behind the 'Upside Down Organisation Chart' (see chapter 6). The greatest leaders lead – but they also serve.

But what does that feel like? What does it actually mean in the real world? I have already talked about defending your team ferociously if need be. I have talked about only venting when you are one-on-one. I have mentioned the best way to lead, teach and mentor. I have talked about being positive but realistic. I guess I could use that old platitude of 'never ask them to do something you won't do yourself'. Even if you do all of that is there still more? Perhaps you can think of a teacher or someone who influenced your early life? What was it about them that inspired you? I bet it wasn't that they did the basics and by the book, was it? I would like to share three personal examples with you. Two that I experienced, one that is an example of my own approach.

First Example

It is MANY years ago and as a young 6 year-old boy I went to Sunday School. My teacher was an elderly lady called Hilda Woodford. She was great. One day she was teaching us about being reliable and loyal. All of a sudden, she jumped up and said "Right, get your coats on, we are going out." I guess there were about ten of us in the class. Sitting outside church was a black taxi-cab. She opened the door and we all climbed in. Of course, this was a long, long time before health and safety rules. Once crammed in tight, off we went. The taxi drove for about 15 minutes until we drew up alongside a small statue (see below). It was Greyfriars Bobby, the incredibly famous dog who sat at his master's graveside for many years after he died. A Hollywood film was made of this very touching, true story. She gathered us around and recounted the story, pointing to the little statue. Then we jumped back in the taxi and back to church. When we left church and all started gabbling to our parents about taxis and dogs they were totally confused! But, six decades later do I still remember that lesson? Well, you know the answer to that one! Here's a very quick summary of the story we were retold on that day. *"Greyfriars Bobby (May 4, 1855 – January 14, 1872) was a Skye Terrier who became known in 19th-century Edinburgh for spending 14 years guarding the grave of his owner until he died himself on 14 January 1872."* Rubbing the statue's nose has become a good luck tradition for visitors as you can see by the shine.

Second Example
At the start of the book I placed a picture of myself in my first team – a young football (soccer) team. Now, I want to move forward a generation. My youngest son Tom was desperate to play football too. He wanted to join a club and learn more about football. By pure chance and good luck, he himself contacted Hutchison Vale Football Club (commonly known in Scotland as 'Hutchie Vale') and was accepted on trial. After a while he was signed up by them and played there for several years. Now, think of your own childhood sporting activity. Hutchie turned out to be

a SERIOUS amateur club. They have been a 'feeder' for several of the largest professional football clubs in the UK. He thrived there. How special was the teaching, coaching and leadership there? Well, you know that old saying *"A picture is better than 1,000 words"*. Take a few seconds and look at the picture below.

| P:39 | W:37 | D:2 | L:0 | *Hutchison Vale U.13* | For | Against | League Points |
| | | | | *2004-2005* | 238 | 34 | 40 |

Think of any sport you follow. This team, in their world, played 39 games and won 37. They drew the other two. Unbeaten for a full year. They scored 238 goals and only conceded 34 in the league. What's more, they won (deep breath) the following knock-out tournaments –

1. Edinburgh City Cup
2. Eastern Region Cup
3. Ken Ritchie Cup
4. Lothian Buses Cup
5. Steve Maskrey Cup
6. Tom Welsh Cup
7. And last, but definitely not least, THE Scottish Cup.

Yes, they were officially the best team in the country, beating the youth teams from all the big major-league professional clubs and the best boys' clubs – every time, in every competition, for that whole year. (Tom is kneeling on the front row, second from the right)

Were the players all just, by chance, incredible? No. Some went on to greater things but most just continued to enjoy playing for fun in later life. What made the difference? In my opinion, just two things. First, the ethos and culture of the club. Train hard and win easy. Train more than the competition. Learn the techniques, skills and science. Second, of course, the coaching and personal mentoring. Led, in this case by Alec Robertson (on the left), an unpaid, amateur coach who achieved all of the above. Supported by Frank Lewis (on the right). Do you think Tom and I will remember them for life?

Third Example
No pictures this time, sorry. I was leading a team that was starting to go places. In fact, it is the team I mentioned in chapter 7 – after leaving the company where my manager didn't acknowledge a big success. It became a team tradition, when we won a really large deal, against the odds, for everyone to go for lunch – and I mean everyone in the office. Now this was a branch of a big multinational company. We had a receptionist, administrators, trainers as well as the sales and pre-sales teams. Lunch often then went on – and on – and on – right onto the end of the night sometimes, and beyond.

So, I would go along for the lunch then head back to the office. I would deal with the outbound post, answer calls and cover the reception desk! I would close up the office. Was this stupid, idiotic, nonsense? Oh, make no mistake, I was still the boss and yes, non-performing staff did leave the company under my watch. BUT I also wanted to lead by example. And when the occasion arose, I did. In fact, a couple of times, my wife came into town and did the same so I could stay longer with the team! Loyalty, desire for success and work-rate deserve reward. Not just for the sales team. These small extra steps – just like the football coach and Sunday School teacher remain in the mind of individuals long after the work role - and even the company itself - have ended.

The Lesson

Lead from the front, set the example and just do the right thing. Don't be superior or aloof. Don't consider yourself a better human just because of your job role. I bet you that if you think back on your worst ever boss, you could picture the exact opposite of those three examples above. Well, at least the first two!

"Leaders instil in their people a hope for success and a belief in themselves. Positive leaders empower people to accomplish their goals."

Anonymous

Notes

_____

_____

_____

_____

_____

_____

_____

_____

_____

_____

_____

_____

_____

_____

_____

_____

_____

_____

_____

_____

_____

Chapter

29

Simplify

"For the overachievers out there. Your mantra is likely 'what else can I do today?' Consider replacing that for a week with, 'what can I do less of today?' and see what happens..."

Ted Hargrave

How is life for you these days? I would make a guess that in business, possibly in family, definitely in your country and society, things are getting more and more complex, pretty well every day.

I have watched this trend closely for around 30 years now. Many years ago, I bought a cassette tape (yes, that many years ago!) on the subject of improving my sales. I could put it into my tape drive as I drove my gold Ford Cortina around the UK. A wondrous car at that time. The sales guru from the US (name long forgotten) talked about the increasing complexity of life. He talked about complexity and connections. In other words, every year, you make more connections, your life becomes more complicated and the outside world is also becoming more and more complex at the same time, sometimes even faster. He said *"If your life is getting simpler, I want to meet you".*

He was right at that time. And for every year since. Life has continued relentlessly to become ever more complex. In fact, there is a current hit TV show in the UK (on BBC, worth a watch if you can find it online) called 'Going Back for the Weekend'. A modern family who live in London, in a terraced, older house, are the guinea pigs. They are removed from their own home, it is remodelled and redecorated – 100% to a specific decade - and then they are dropped back in along with an instruction book and they have to live there exactly as they would have done in that decade. It is fascinating. But it really brought this whole concept back to me. The series starts in the 1950's with them having to live for real at a rate of a day per year, so 10 days to cover the decade. But, just wow! The 1950's home... Main living room; coal fire, three seats, one table and a radio. That was it. It brings our lives today into focus with a vengeance. And as each decade progresses in the show you can see the wealth, relative luxury, complexity and material goods continue to grow and grow.

What about the business world? Gertrude Stein said this *"Everybody gets so much information all day long that they lose their common sense."* We are working under a deluge of choices, information, access to more information and suggestions in every aspect of business life. We need to simplify. I have already discussed your priorities and time management. But how about consciously simplifying your working life? Start with your core priorities. Then ask yourself what else can be removed? Or delegated? Or delayed? Or reduced and simplified in itself. With simplicity comes time to focus and time to improve your performance. Teach the idea to your team members too. Here's a great question for them (which can be easily adapted to any other area of work). *"Last week, how much time out of your total working time, was spent on your core sales activities – speaking to prospects, cold calling, moving prospects along your pipeline, delivering presentations and proposals?"* I bet the best answer – if truthful – is less than 50%, and often a lot, lot less.

The Lesson
Simplicity is better. It is also easier and delivers greater focus. It gives you that time to react and to consider. In the UK we say *"you can't see the woods for the trees".* Is that you today?

"It is not a daily increase, but a daily decrease. Hack away at the inessentials."

Bruce Lee

Notes

Chapter

30

Unfair
Mindshare

"Creativity is one of the last remaining ways of gaining an unfair advantage over the competition."

Ed McCabe

The concept of Unfair Mindshare in sales is one I came up with myself many years ago. Again, it can be applied in any area of endeavour...

I have spent my whole working life working for incredible companies. BUT every single one was the #2 or #3 – or even lower - in its marketplace. I have never worked for the largest player or market leader. This means that year after year I was having to do more, sell better, strengthen and support my team, create a 'bow-wave' and somehow stand out. I became successful at winning against the odds and eventually gave the things I did a name – 'Unfair Mindshare'.

On carrying out a quick search today on Goggle, I found no one else using the exact same terminology in the same context. A couple of articles talked about similar concepts. But I am not at all precious about the phrase, it's just the wording I came up with to reflect my experience and success.

What exactly is Unfair Mindshare and how and where can it be used?

Imagine you are leading a start-up, SME or sales team. You don't have the scale or reach of the bigger, more established players. What can you do? Well, first you have to make sure that your strategy and execution are world class. You have to be active, reaching out and using every technique and tool I have described, both in this book and The B2B Selling Guidebook. But you can do more...

1. **Be available.** Those who write and comment on technology, or indeed, any other market speciality or local news source are creatures of habit. They are human. Reach out personally to the writers and editors of every single journal, magazine, bulletin and blog that impacts your market and/or geography. Explain very simply, the sort of knowledge you bring to the table AND the top two or three uniques your

organisation brings to its market or geography. Yes, even if you are only a branch operation (but maybe run the finished content past your HQ marketing in this case). Offer your services to them. Give them a 'freebie' article and let them take ownership so they don't have to work to create anything. Even not directly mentioning your organisation – just a good, short article commenting on your specific sector. Once that is done stay in touch. Drop them snippets and press releases. Be friendly and available. You see, everyone who creates content never, ever, has enough time. Short cuts, trusted sources for quotes, friendly contacts are a massive benefit to them. Once you have offered and then delivered value, you can go in their 'black book'. I have done this for over 20 years. Each time I have done it, around 50% of those I went through that first phase with then started to use me for information, quotes and guest articles. Suddenly, you aren't a small player, you are a thought leader! And you can also be working away on your own blog, White Paper and/or podcast series too. I have seen them being picked up and quoted verbatim once I had those relationships. You are now bigger and more influential to the outside world than you 'deserve' to be. *Unfair Mindshare.*

2. **The Big Boys.** Once you have achieved the first step above, you can go after the big boys. On my own (or working closely with a very small, but high quality PR agency) I have been able to reach and gain personal and company coverage from UK organisations such as The Financial Times, The Daily Telegraph, the biggest industry journals, the BBC's flagship 'Breakfast' TV programme and the Sky TV (UK's biggest digital channel) Technology programme. Seeing the quality of your output and comments for the lower tiers can give you a small step up in reaching out to these big beasts. And they

each also have the same time and output pressures. You have to bring strong opinion, a powerful new message or similar but it can really work if you do. Doing this multiplies your impact and presence. Your organisation is now hitting away above its weight in the market. Oh, and BTW, this coverage is satisfying at a personal level, really upsets your competitors and is a powerful help for you, when you do decide to move to pastures new. *Unfair Mindshare.*

3. **Take the High Ground.** Let's say you inhabit a fiercely competitive market sector. But you are nowhere near the largest or dominant. Sit down with your team and look at what areas or measures you might lead in. Perhaps it's a product capability, maybe it's the number of consumers or users you have, or it could be that you operate in a 'sub niche' or even that you have introduced a service or capability earlier than anyone else. Now, list them in order of importance to your customers. IF they exist (say, at least two of these items) and you can seriously <u>stand behind</u> your claims then you have a chance to have a lot of fun and create marketplace Unfair Mindshare. Take your presence – perhaps your website front page, core Powerpoint presentation, blog header – or all of them - and change the title from the usual marketing statements to something like... "By several measures, Acme is the market leader in the xxxxx sector." Say it loud and repeat it often. Two things typically happen. First, you get far more coverage, then secondly, and this has amused me each time I have done it, your competitors start to tell their contacts to ignore you because you aren't really the market leader, they are! Now, if you are a customer or prospect and the biggest supplier specifically names someone they are obviously worried about, what is the first thing you would do? Yes, look that other organisation up and read about them. So, there was an initial

increase in traffic and inbound contacts, followed by an acceleration as our competition did our marketing work for us. Unfair Mindshare.

4. **Drip, drip, drip.** Once you have made contact with an important new prospect look at how you can move to 'front of centre' with them. How many ways can you communicate? Which ways do they prefer? LinkedIn? Facebook? Podcast? White papers? Personal ideas and/or notes by email? Now – for that prospect – set out a communication plan. What will you communicate? When? Using what medium? Get it into your diary with a reminder, or in your CRM 'action notes'. Then deliver content that is thoughtful, interesting, delivering value and ideas. If you do this, only with content and ideas tuned to their challenges, they will start to look for the next one – in much the same way as in the story from my first book, below. *Unfair Mindshare.*

5. **Awards.** In every market, city, geography and vertical sector there are bodies who create awards programmes – usually on an annual basis. Find out every single one that exists, that you could enter. Then, using some of the principles above and as many strong customer quotes as you can, complete a strong entry for every single one. My personal success record? Six award wins in one year! Over the last 20 years I have achieved a success rate of around 40%. Even being recognized as a finalist is newsworthy. It doesn't take a lot of time; the ceremonies are usually fun to attend and the rewards and publicity and presence can be phenomenal. You see, as I now realise, all of these awards programmes are also competing with each other so they go all out to gain as much publicity and coverage as they can for their big night and their winners. A double win. *Unfair Mindshare.*

6. **Bits of Paper.** Not all unfair mindshare actions have to involve much effort or outlay. The simplest I have seen? A company I worked with, a fantastic sales and marketing 'engine', set out a simple, standard action to increase awareness. Every time a deal was won, they would visit the customer site afterwards and leave a big stack of one-page (perhaps half the size of A4 or Legal sized paper) sheets that were titled 'Your Project and Account Team'. The header was the logos of both companies. It then listed the direct contact information for everyone who any individual within the customer might conceivably want to contact. Sales, pre-sales, support, training, marketing, administration, finance. Often it was every single individual in the local branch. But as an employee in the customer, when you looked at it you just saw a very long list of people who were your own, dedicated, supplier project team. The psychology was fantastic. In customer after customer I would see that sheet stuck up on the cubicle dividers everywhere I went. People saw it every day, your 'large team' dedicated to them was there every day – and individually named. And of course, our logo, top line motto and branding were also there every day too. So easy, so powerful. *Unfair Mindshare.*

7. **Your Address.** Many start-ups and smaller organisations share their building with other companies. Or they are in 'managed office centres'. Look at your address. Does it say "Suite 10" or "Unit 6" or "Room 5" or similar? Check with the reception, estate manager and/or your postal provider. If post and visitors would still find you OK, then just drop that "Suite 10" part of your address. Doesn't "The Alpha Building" sound a lot better than "Suite 10, The Alpha Building"? I have done this multiple times - deliveries, visitors and post still arrived fine but the world felt my organisations were just bigger... *Unfair Mindshare.*

The above points all relate to gaining Unfair Mindshare externally. But you can apply the same principles to gain more positive attention, support and visibility for your team internally within a larger organisation too. Here's a really simple example from my first book –

"The story is told of a salesperson working in a large organisation. She wanted to stand out internally because salespeople were looked down on by many in the company. So, every time she worked with administrators or needed their help, she treated them like internal customers. After every trip she would bring back something by way of a (very small) memento and chat to them about what she had done and learned. Step by step she gained their trust and support. THEN, having done this, she bought a box of bright pink paper. Now, every time she put in an internal request or submitted her expenses, she printed them on that paper. Instantly, the rest of the business knew that pink meant her. That was 'Pavlovian conditioning'. While colleagues had long delays in getting what they needed and even in getting their expenses paid, she found everything was going very smoothly for her! While paper might not be the medium today, you can surely see how this same principle could be applied in your world..."

The Lesson
Sit down, review your internal and external potential for some Unfair Mindshare actions, then go for it. It's fun, highly productive and seriously annoys your competitors and rivals. Perfect!

"If you don't have a competitive advantage, don't compete."
Jack Welch

Notes

_____

_____

_____

_____

_____

_____

_____

_____

_____

_____

_____

_____

_____

_____

_____

_____

_____

_____

_____

_____

_____

_____

Chapter

31

Why Worry?

*"Worrying is like a rocking chair –
it gives you something to do,
but it gets you nowhere."*

Vicky Pattison

This is a short, but important chapter...

Sometimes your work becomes everything. It's never out of your head, you are checking emails late at night, you are looking at internal systems in the evening at home, your brain keeps on and on churning over work even when you are supposed to be focussing on other things. This is not good. This is, to be absolutely specific, BAD. This is not sustainable.

At various times in my career I have been there big time. That giant deal took over my life. I couldn't stop thinking of that really difficult team member. Why were our revenues not where they should be? That throwaway comment from the big boss just will not go away. What did she mean, am I in trouble? I bet you can think of a long list of your own examples.

After 43 years of living in a high-pressure environment I have learned a few things from continually getting it wrong. Please just trust me if this is you, you need to focus and read this chapter carefully and thoughtfully.

Rule 1. Work is work. You are a manager and hopefully, a leader. That does not mean that work has to overpower everything else in life. If you have to work more than standard hours do two things. First, as you leave the office (see chapter 16) take conscious steps to switch off. Write down everything you have to do tomorrow and then close the notebook, lock it away, switch off your computer. Consciously switch off and close down.

Rule 2. But I am busy! If, as often happens, you have to work more than standard hours then do the same again. Before you go to bed, set a routine of switching off, making more notes if you need to and closing a notebook or whatever medium you use before you try to rest.

Rule 3. Get a life! I don't care what it is, do something else apart from work and sleep. Exercise, reading (non work related!), socialising, study a skill or hobby, watch sport, grow something. What it is for you doesn't matter, having another life and interest does.

Rule 4. Don't worry! Worrying too much destroys and can kill. If an issue is bearing down on you do all of the above. Then, ask yourself some questions. *"In 10 years will I remember this as a big issue?". "Will others remember it in 10 years too?". "Is it actually more important than the rest of my work, or life, or family?".* Yes, think about it, but also put it in context. Guess what, in my experience I can't even remember now what the crises were in any given year. They are long lost history. Some of them were gigantic challenges and problems. But, with the benefit of hindsight, I can't even recall the details now. Never let a worry, problem or challenge overcome you. At worst, if it is work and it can't be solved and is impacting your health, walk away. And yes, before you ask, I have done exactly that.

Rule 5. Sleep. Yes, take time to get rest. You might think you can power through but over time your performance and ability will drop substantially if you don't get enough recharge time.

Rule 6. Get your Priorities Right. Under extreme pressure how can you respond and function well and work through things if you haven't taken care of yourself through exercise, good food and sleep, looked after or stayed in frequent touch with your family (the most important thing) and taken some me time too. All work and no play make Jim a malfunctioning boy.

For further reading if this is a seriously big problem for you, let me make an 'off the wall' recommendation. Ant Middleton has become a very well-known celebrity in the UK. A former Marine and Special Boat Service (SBS) operator he has seen 'a little more' stress than most. He has climbed Everest. He has fought in many, often unnamed fields of conflict. And then he was overcome by fear. I have recently read his second book, 'The Fear Bubble'. It shows, in great detail, his challenges and the problems they caused, followed by the specific method he created to overcome them. The message is incredibly powerful. His own technique for directly overcoming fear and worry is well worth the price of the book alone. And in my experience, practical and useful for all who worry too.

The Lesson
Don't worry, be happy, as the song goes...

"Worrying is using your imagination to create something you don't want."
Abraham Hicks

Notes

_____

_____

_____

_____

_____

_____

_____

_____ `

_____

_____

_____

_____

_____

_____

_____

_____

_____

_____

_____

_____

_____

_____

_____

_____

Chapter

32 | Attitude and Ethics in Leadership

"Your actions define your character, your words define your wisdom, but your treatment of others defines the REAL you."

Mayur Ramgir

Hands up everyone who has had a boss or CXO level person lie to or mislead them? I simply can't stand dishonesty. It's stupid, its ignorant and it's very short-term, self-defeating behaviour.

Rant over, *"and breathe"...*

As I was saying before I interrupted myself ☺. Your attitude and ethics will stand long after the details of your actions are remembered.

Ask anyone who has worked for a business or corporation to talk about the people there they remember most. I would estimate that seven times out of ten they will say something like *"There was this person. They were so incompetent. They lied all the time. But they got found out in the worst possible way, let me tell you...".* Or *"My boss shouted every day"* or *"I thought I could trust my line manager and then I found that...".* Sometimes, more positively, the overriding memory is of that one great person who they looked up to then and who they will always remember. I have worked for more than a few of both types over the years.

Which category do you want to be in? How do you want to be remembered? And even more important, how do you want to look back on your working life? A bit embarrassed at some of the things you have done? Not wanting to talk about it? Or, happy to recount the ups and downs and to be able to tell anyone with no fear?

This might all sound of little importance to you today. *"Just do whatever you have to win".* But let me assure you, as time goes on, it's the things you did wrong that keep on coming back. In recent years I have reached out to a couple of people I believe I wronged to repair damage. Now that's a good feeling when completed.

Again, you have to set your own path and style. But, for what it is worth, I believe very strongly that nothing is important enough to make you forgo your principles and beliefs. You will just be unhappy and less effective if you do. Sure, in the short term you might make things easier for yourself. But even in the medium or longer term – if not in the short term anyway – you will feel better, be in more control and working better if you stick to what you know is right.

A positive attitude, clear ethics and behavioural expectations, combined with leading by example is a 100% common theme among those leaders I can now look back on with warmth and respect. Make sure your legacy is on the right side of history!

In recent months I have become interested in, and impressed by, the Japanese concept of Ikigai. In the West we seem to take numbers and objectives as 'everything'. Ikigai accepts that but then adds in other elements to achieve real fulfilment. Put simply, Ikigai (as shown in the diagram below) means 'your reason for being'. It is the combination of having a purpose in life, one that is more rounded than just the measurables. Four elements combine to achieve Ikigai – passion, vocation, profession and mission. If you can find a place where what you love connects to what you are actually good at, and at the same time, links to what you can be paid for and the world needs – then you are in a great place. It's a lovely, simplistic way of looking at life overall. I hope the diagram resonates for you. (thanks to 'Claudette S' for this particular version of the diagram)

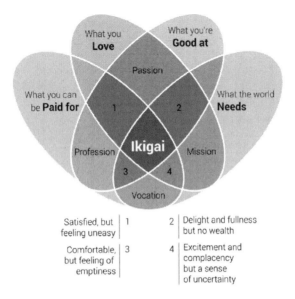

Satisfied, but feeling uneasy	1	2	Delight and fullness but no wealth
Comfortable, but feeling of emptiness	3	4	Excitement and complacency but a sense of uncertainty

Finally, on this point, above my desk I have the following quote – *"The three grand essentials of happiness are: something to do, someone to love, and something to hope for"* by Alexander Chalmers.

I spent two long chapters in The B2B Selling Guidebook reflecting and advising on ethics and behaviour in both your working life and private life and I do not intend to repeat those here.

Except for one very short quote –

Many years ago, I was driving and listening to BBC Radio. The news programme had a 'Thought for the Day' delivered each day by a different religious or moral leader. On this day, the speaker had been the manager of one of the UK's largest hospices – someone who had literally helped many thousands of people come to terms with and prepare for the end of their life. A fantastic life's work dedicated to helping others. After his 2-minute talk was finished the newsreader broke with tradition (usually just moving straight back to the news with no comment) and asked him if he had any other thoughts. The speaker thought for a second then just said *"Well, I can say this. Of all the people I have met over the past 20 years as they came to the end of their lives, not one has ever said "I wish I had spent more time in the office..." Step back and really ask yourself, what are my true priorities?".*

The Lesson
In the middle of the maelstrom that is life, decide and act on your own principles, attitudes and ethics. Always be true to yourself.

"To be an ethical leader is indeed to be different. This kind of leader acknowledges the complexity of running a responsible business, yet tries to do it anyway."

Andrew Leigh

Notes

_____

_____

_____

_____

_____

_____

_____

_____

_____

_____

_____

_____

_____

_____

_____

_____

_____

_____

_____

_____

_____

_____

Chapter

33 Summary

*"If I had to live my life again,
I'd make the same mistakes,
only sooner!"*

Tallulah Bankhead

So here we are.

I hope you have enjoyed the journey with me. I can tell you; I have enjoyed creating it for you. Now, I don't expect you to agree with everything I have written. If you did, I would be confused and disappointed. But I truly do hope that at least some of the chapters have resonated with you.

Having laid down the chapter titles I then just typed, in a 'stream of consciousness' style. Now I can, like you, for the first time, read the whole book myself.

If you are an old hand maybe I have reminded you of some basics. If you are new to leadership, just opening your dream start-up, running an SME or getting that much deserved promotion to management I hope this short book can be both an influence today and, more important, something you can leaf through every once in a while.

If the book sits on your shelf, fully or part read and still pristine I will be disappointed. I would love to see pages folded over, underlining, asterisks, markings and highlighted sections. That's all I ask from you. Disagree a lot if you want but where you find something new or powerful, don't just read and carry on, mark it and then adopt it!

As I read it all back, what do I think is worth putting in this summary. What lessons, in retrospect, do I most value? Here we go –

- Work at learning to both lead and manage. It's very rare for it just to happen spontaneously.

- Be consistent in your approach and manner. Stability breeds confidence and trust.

- PLAN! First impressions, strategies, goals and actions.

- Always be aware of the context, the people involved and your environment as you lead.

- Be clear. Don't leave room for doubt. When the challenge, the task, the goal or the discipline is absolutely clear, then the team can work to achieve that more easily – even if they don't like it.

- Create an identity for your company, division or team. Stand apart and be different.

- Delegate whenever and whatever you reasonably can. It eases your burden, gives your team responsibility and helps them develop.

- It is always your business – so own it.

- Focus on asking good, in depth questions. With your team, your peers, your leaders and customers. Strong questions deliver better answers.

- Take input from every possible source, then act fast.

- Always think of the individual; their life, their issues, their potential.

- Never stop coaching and mentoring your team.

- You are only as effective as your time management. Be rigorous yourself and do the same for your team. Are the stated goals and priorities being put first?

- Always be a positive force, but don't be shy about disciplining quickly and firmly when you have to.

- Lead by example. Prove you are their leader, not just 'a manager'.

- You will never be able to control what happens to

you. But you can always control how you respond. Don't worry about what the world will dump on you, concentrate on how you react.

- Live a customer centric, focused and service led business life. No customers? No business. Less customers? Less money and ability to succeed. And don't ever forget your internal customers.

- Don't just be a robot. Laugh, chat, encourage, support every time it's right or appropriate.

- In your market and also internally within a larger organisation, focus continually on what will deliver you ever more Unfair Mindshare.

- Keep learning! Always...

- And finally, have a life! Work is not, should not and never will be, everything in life.

"Maybe all one can do is hope to end up with the right regrets."

Arthur Miller

Jim Irving
November 2020

Notes

Appendix 1

Suggested Reading

Here are just a few books and sources that I think can be useful to you as you consider leadership, management, sales and marketing. There is no 'this is best', look at the area you are interested in and then scan each of these online for your own fit. But I recommend them all...

"Great things are done by a series of small things brought together."

Vincent Van Gogh

Sales Books and sources

- The B2B Selling Guidebook by Jim Irving. Well, I had to, didn't I... ☺
- Unlocking Yes, Perpetual Hunger & The Bonus Round by Patrick Tinney
- Anything by Jeb Blount
- Funnel Vision by Steve Knapp
- Secrets of Successful Sales by Alison Edgar
- Everybody Works in Sales and The Easy Guide to Sales for Business Owners by Niraj Kapur
- Posts, blogs, websites and podcasts by all of the above plus the likes of Anthony Iannarino, Herb Cohen, Jeremy Jacobs, Colly Graham, Daniel Disney and Simon Hares

Marketing Books

- Anything by Al Ries and Jack Trout
- Anything by Seth Godin
- The Internet Marketing Bible by Zeke Camusio
- Marketing Management by Philip Kotler
- Guerrilla Marketing by Jay Levinson
- Crushing It by Gary Vaynerchuk

Business Books

- The Tipping Point and Outliers by Malcolm Gladwell
- Grit by Angela Duckworth
- 7 Habits of Highly Effective People by Stephen R Covey
- Crossing the Chasm by Geoffrey Moore
- Built to Last and Good to Great by James Collins (and Jerry Porras)
- In Search of Excellence by Tom Peters
- The Art of War by Sun Tzu

"Learn continually – there's always 'one more thing' to learn!"

Steve Jobs

Appendix 2
A Fuller List of Recent Reviews/ Feedback on The B2B Selling Guidebook

"We all need people who will give us feedback. That's how we improve."

Bill Gates

Amazon Reviews

"Compelling, insightful reading... this book is a great example of the wealth of experience that he has amassed throughout his career. Poignant in parts, it provides a real-life view of Jim's 40+ year sales career and he touches on the highs and lows of selling, using very clear examples to make each point... I can't recommend this book highly enough if you're in any way involved in sales, or if you're interested in learning more about the everyday challenges that those of us in this noble profession face."

Colin

"Absolutely the most practical and useful book ever written on B2B selling." "From beginning to end, Jim Irving's masterpiece is simplistically instructive but also captivating. This book is powered by Jim's 40+ years of selling experience. It's a shortcut through the hard knocks route of mastering the crazy nuances of the B2B selling profession. Highly recommend this book and this author."

Tkadams30 (USA)

"A book that should be read by anyone in any business discipline". "... Jim brings years of business experience to the table in what should become the bible for anyone in any business discipline where there is a focus on B2B markets." "...Jim cuts to the chase with real anecdotal evidence from his vast experience which saw him rise to the very top of the tough global industry sector within which he worked. And it works when put into practice! I am seeing the actual results right now in my business life. Jim is a hero and his book is a must-read."

Amazon Customer

"The sales book you have always been looking for." "... Unlike many other b2b books, Jim breaks down sales strategies and turns them into understandable stories rather than dry theory. Think of this book as the university of life version of a four-year degree on selling. I challenge anyone, whether new to sales or a 20-year veteran, to read this book and not come away with practical ways to be a better sales person. It'll be the best thing you've ever bought under a tenner."

John G Ferris

"Real stories and advice to accelerate your sales, no matter your experience or skillset." "I have had the pleasure of working with Jim and it had a huge impact on my career and success. This book pulls together everything you need to know about sales and making your customers happy. It covers all aspects to help accelerate your revenues. If you want to sell better, faster and generate more revenue for your business and career...get this book today."

Grainne

"Regardless of your experience, you need this book." "As a seasoned, long in the tooth sales professional and sales trainer, I have read a lot of stuff, mostly rubbish and one or two real gems. This book is in the latter category. Experienced sales professionals look to learn from other seasoned professionals for our development. We don't want theory we want relatable experience that can be applied first hand. That's what you get in this book. In 2020 B2B sales needs to be effective, especially with Covid-19. This book felt like a safe pair of hands and I truly recommend you read it."

Simon Hares, SerialTrainer7 Ltd

"Different, insightful, compelling read based on real world experience." "Unlike any other corporate sales book, you will ever read. I had the privilege of working for "Gentlemen Jim" in the early 2000's and this book explains his grounded approach to Sales... Any salesperson adopting just one of Jim's learnings here will find a genuine shortcut to success. The only comment I might make is about the title. It's not a guide at all but an insight into the mind, experience and thinking behind one of the most respected executives from the UK IT industry in the last 40 years. An outstanding read and an even better listen from the author's own voice in the audio recording."

Paul

"Must read! Up there with the best." "I've read 20+ books about sales over the last year, this is one of the best. Jim takes a different approach from most sales books in the way he formats each short chapter. Each one starts with an introduction of a principle, an example of how Jim has applied this in a high-level sales situation, followed by a summary of the lesson learned. The anecdotes are interesting and funny at times which really helps visualise how to handle various sales situations. Unlike a lot of sales books, the principles learned from The B2B Guidebook apply very well to C-level selling. When you read Jim's career history and references from C-level and Director level people, you know that the man is worth paying attention to."

Martin Tonothy

Other Reviews

"Pick up a copy of this amazing enterprise selling book and break out the highlighters!!" "I have just finished reading 'The B2B Selling Guidebook' by author Jim Irving. It is clear Jim is a big-time money-ball seller. His enterprise selling stories and business cases are moving and motivating. It is clear author Irving wants to leave something personal for the business community. His ideas are crystal clear and worth repeating. Pick up a copy and break out the high lighters!"

Patrick Tinney, World famous author of 'Perpetual Hunger' and other sales classics.

"The selling process offers a peep-hole into the human condition. In this book, Jim helps the sales person see reality, develop insights and then, most of all, add long-term value to the client-supplier relationship."

Bob Bishop, Former Chairman & CEO, Silicon Graphics Inc

Institute of Sales Management

"Irving writes in a clear, down to earth style. He is not so much teaching you but sharing ideas in the same way a sales manager might mentor a salesperson. Overall, it's a good read for any salesperson. Entrepreneurs looking to increase their sales will also find the book of value. The book is recommended for anyone looking for ideas on how to increase their knowledge about sales practice without a substantial time commitment."

ISM Winning Edge Magazine, July 2020. Reviewer – Roger Bradburn, COO and Director

Chartered Institute of Marketing

"In 'The B2B Selling Guidebook', Jim Irving sets out many of the fundamentals of professional and ethical selling. Jim is a CIM Fellow and a Fellow of the Institute of Sales Management. His 43-year career encompasses leadership roles in both disciplines. The book covers the most important sales lessons of his career. Each short, enjoyable chapter takes a sales attribute or discipline, explains it through real-life stories and then delivers insight to the reader." ... with powerful lessons for all." www.cim.co.uk

CIM Catalyst Magazine, July 2020 edition. Reviewer – John Knapton

"Jim Irving beats me. His 40+ years vs my 34 in B2B sales... Read it... regardless of your time served you will learn and you will be challenged... The B2B Selling Guide Book is so well thought through as Jim provides you with one insight and example after another. I really enjoyed the quotes, the lessons and the notes pages that turn this into a workbook to take around with you... This book takes its place in the PLAN. GROW. DO. Ltd recommendations that support our sales training."

Steve Knapp, The Sales Mindset Coach, author of "Funnel Vision"

"Complete with an exclamation mark, 'keep learning' are the final two words of this excellent book by Jim Irving. Like a stick of Margate or Blackpool rock, those two words are weaved through all twenty-one chapters. Aimed at seasoned salespeople as well as novices, this little black book is a cornucopia of sales content and personal anecdotes from Jim's forty plus years in sales. The entire book is written in Plain English (a pleasant change) and there are some excellent appendices at the back. I'm reading this book again I liked it so much."

Jeremy Jacobs, The Sales Rainmaker

Discovery Books Website

"I found the format of this book unique and interesting..." "The author writes in simple language that makes it easy for people with no experience in sales to understand the subject." "I think this makes the book a well-rounded work for anyone who wants to learn about B2B selling." "I found this book informative, interesting and easy to understand."

Discovery Books, (see www.reedsy.com/discovery). Professional Reviewer – Satabdi Mukherjee

Appendix 3
Comments on Jim Irving's Leadership Credentials

"True intuitive expertise is learned from prolonged experience with good feedback on mistakes."

Daniel Kahneman

"Jim is a seasoned sales leader with a proven track record of success in multiple channels and business models. His leadership and motivation skills elevate the productivity of his teams resulting in consistently exceeded goals. He is respected by his customers, team, peers, and senior management."

Greg Goelz, President & CEO, Smart Locus Inc, Californian

"I first met Jim when I asked him to be the MD of a technology company I chaired. He brought clarity and strong execution to the business and massively increased market visibility while improving business results and motivating staff. He delivers very strong sales and communication skills to every endeavour"

Michael Black MBE, Successful technology entrepreneur. Non-Executive Director at Danske Bank, Non-Executive Director at Titan IC Systems and Chairman – Displaynote Technologies

"Jim is an excellent leader who manages to combine the strength of character, determination and toughness that's required to fulfil senior roles with his great kindness, warmth and humility. He also brings his huge experience and wealth of skills to bear in a hands-on manner and was an excellent manager to work for. I would gladly recommend him to anyone."

Gary Baverstock, Sales Director Northern Europe, Denodo Technologies

"I worked with Jim whilst heading up pre-sales in a regional branch of a major US multinational. The branch had underperformed for several years and Jim was promoted to lead it. The change in style that Jim brought was questioned by some to start but over 2 years the region went from bottom in the UK to top and #2 in Europe. Jim's 'serving to lead' approach turned a group of individuals into a high performing team. It was incredibly effective."

Mike Robb, founder of independent IT consultancy, Avendris

"Turning around a broken sales organization, one with a culture of underperformance and lethargy is a monumental challenge. In short order, Jim took a bottom-dwelling country operation and grew it to one of the best performing teams in the world. His no-frills, straightforward and ethical approach to building a world-class sales organization is something to this day that I not only admire, but also strive to emulate."

David Rode, Former Senior Vice President, International Operations, Information Builders (IBI)

"Jim's reputation is very well established. He has gone in to lead sales/the business in difficult circumstances and markets and has delivered clarity in strategy and also in sales execution and improved results. He understands the dynamics of selling."

Professor Paul Atkinson, Founding Partner - Par Equity (a multi award winning VC firm), Executive Chairman Taranata Group and serial investor

"Jim is a natural sales leader, able to instantly command attention and respect from both his sales team and prospective clients. He has a relaxed and friendly approach which puts customers at ease and gains their trust. This, coupled with a keen commercial drive, enables him to identify opportunity, develop winning sales arguments and effectively manage the sales process to ensure his team make their numbers."

Ian Baxter, Vice President - NetDimensions

Appendix 4

Some Thoughts on Selling, Managing and Leading in the Covid-19 World, and After.

"The more things change, the more they remain the same."

Or as originally stated –

"Plus ça change, plus c'est la même chose."

Jean-Baptiste Alphonse Karr (in 1849!)

It is fair to say that you could describe me as *"an old hand for a new world".* I do have some definite views on the very different world we are in right now.

As I wrote this book, I realised that a lot of what I have learned is about coping with change. Change can, of course, occur in every sphere of life. From the point that I started the book the world has indeed changed – and in so many ways. Covid-19 has created and forced incredible levels of change everywhere and as I complete my writing it still wreaks havoc around the world. What is my take on it and the impact it does – and will – have on all of us? Let me start with some context...

One advantage of my very long business life is that I have experienced real, serious, disruptive change several times now. For me, some of the biggest situations were the following –

- Massive inflation over a long period of time (price rises on everything EVERY week) during one economic crisis.

- The '3-day week crisis' in the UK. Political strife created an environment where the working week was reduced to just three days. Electricity and everything it provided was simply cut off on a regular basis. I worked by candle-light!

- The forced devaluation of the £ with all that it involved.

- Personal crises – health and others

What have I learned? The first response I make is one that I covered in depth in The B2B Selling Guidebook. Without going through the whole story, it is this. *"This too will pass".* At the best of times, the worst of times and everything in between, always know that *"this too will pass".* Things WILL change again as they always have and always will.

Change has been a constant throughout the history of society. While Covid-19 delivers unexpected and enforced change, it is nonetheless, just an extreme example of change.

In chapter 29 ('Simplify') I mentioned the BBC series where a family had to 'live' for real through all the decades from the 1950's. I was really shocked at the scale of the changes since those days, but normally change creeps up on us and we don't notice. Disruptive events – such as Covid-19, earthquakes, 9-11, famines etc have a massive, instant and direct impact on those who experience them, but slowly and gradually after the shock, things start to normalise again. We never forget, but as the rather trite saying states 'life goes on'. And it does.

But everything I have said about crises and change are taken from a relatively comfortable Western viewpoint. Look again at the bullet-point list of those things which impacted me. Each one was difficult and serious to me. But isn't it the case that a large percentage of the world-wide population are experiencing all of these together, right now? I think it is always worth taking our troubles and placing them in context.

But what about the impact of Covid-19 on our business and working lives? Bearing in mind what I have said above, we first need to separate the real challenges from the imagined or inconsequential. If the worst business impact was that meetings were never again going to be face-to-face but by high definition video technology, would we adapt? Of course we would. Relationship building and conversation would become more difficult (as we already know from 'Zoom fatigue') but we would cope. It is possible that science will deliver some solution to Covid-19 (please!) so maybe this issue will be short to medium term only anyway. I do not see these physical challenges as being a major issue.

However, some things will change as long as the current restrictions are in place – in some form. Let's look at selling first...

Selling
The business impact of Covid is simple. It has delivered a major shock to the world-wide economy. When such shocks occur does the business world stop? No! Two things happen. First there are always clear losers and winners, short term. At the moment, the online and home delivery worlds have just exploded with demand. But retail, hospitality, travel and other sectors are being devastated. Second, generally speaking, everywhere that is impacted by the shock becomes MUCH more focussed on value. Money and time is tighter. Life is harder. So selling is also more difficult. I am sure we are all familiar with the concept of the 'gatekeeper'. The receptionist, administrator, secretary or buyer who act to stop us getting to the person we want/need to speak to. It is my belief that now, value itself is another gatekeeper – more than ever before in our business lifetimes. What do I mean? Sales theory has taught that we need to build a relationship based on interest and trust, find out more about the prospect and only then sell. This still holds true. BUT, how do you get their time and attention when they are stressed, under pressure and less interested? You have to show and prove the potential for value up front in order to overcome that hurdle. I found this to be true in those UK crises I lived and worked through. It's also true today. What makes it worth their while giving you time? What examples or reference stories can you deliver right at the start of the conversation? Without value at the fore, life will become ever more difficult. So, focus on your up-front value messaging, think of what their world is right now and respond and communicate accordingly.

Managing and Leading

The section above on selling really says that in the good times almost everyone who is competent and has some form of reasonable service or product can survive or even prosper. The true test is when things get tough. And they are tough today. As a leader this is your time. If you look down, accept defeat and give up, your team will too. Today the burden on you is immense. But you can do it. Life will likely be harder for some time but a focus on being the best, leading/mentoring/supporting your team as well as you possibly can will pay big dividends. Whether your customers are internal or external, focus on understanding them and their world better and tuning and adapting to that as quickly as possible. Work to create new standards for online meetings and demonstrations. Look for ways to excel. In this respect, search online for innovations and ideas. I am joining lots of webcasts and podcasts at the moment. Some are just 'ok', but some give me great ideas! Invest your time in learning so you can lead and educate your team better. At another difficult time I found that having some experience and desire to adapt were invaluable. Do you remember the dot.com boom and bust? During that time, I was a CEO leading a large software business team. I had become used to being headhunted all the time. At the height of dotcom the calls stopped. I knew a few 'players' in that recruitment space and asked them what was happening. *"Oh, it's really easy. No one wants older, experienced heads now, the world has changed and we need young, ideas-based heads to lead today"* they said. In the month after the bust guess what? My phone was ringing off the hook! *"We need experience, we need those who have been through things like this before"* was the new cry. And so it is today. In every geography or marketplace there are experienced people who are willing to give some time and advice – seek them out and ask for their input. It's an easy way to bypass the mistakes and learning for these more difficult times.

In summary, today is more difficult than a year or two ago. But the world has not stopped. Focus, hard work, differentiation and innovation will create success. Work at it!

"If you do not change direction, you may end up where you are heading."

Lao Tzu

"Few things are more important during a change event than communication from leaders who can paint a clear and confidence-inspiring vision of the future"

Sarah Clayton

www.b2bsellingguidebook.com

www.b2bleadersguidebook.com

Printed in Great Britain
by Amazon